Mark Irvine and Marion Cadman

Commercially

Student's Book

OXFORD
UNIVERSITY PRESS

Contents

Introduction

Teresa Volpe

Teresa is Italian. She lives in L'Aquila, a beautiful town in the centre of Italy. She is nineteen and she finished school last month. At school she studied commerce, accounting, mathematics, Italian, and English. She doesn't really know what to do next.

She's qualified to work in an office, but she doesn't want to do that. A lot of her friends want to do business studies at university, but she doesn't want to do any more exams.

Her mother and father want her to look for a good secure job, but she wants to travel for a year to see if she can think of something more exciting. It's not easy to find an interesting job in L'Aquila.

Peter Clapton

Peter is Teresa's Australian cousin. He lives in Melbourne. Peter is twenty-one. He finished school three years ago. He enjoyed school. He studied English, French, social studies, politics, and geography. He is interested in sport and is a volleyball referee in his spare time. One day he would like to referee at international games.

After he left school Peter had a number of jobs. He delivered pizzas, worked in a shoe shop, and served in fast food places. Then he worked for a short time in an import-export office, but he didn't like it very much. He preferred the other jobs because he had more freedom. But he knows he can't deliver pizzas all his life.

Silvia Adario

Silvia is Spanish. She is twenty-four and she lives in Barcelona. After she finished school, she went to a commercial school and got a diploma in commerce.

Three years ago her parents wanted to sell their small gift shop because business was not good. Silvia told them that she could make the shop a success. So, they didn't sell it and Silvia started to manage it. At first she had some difficult times, but now the shop is very popular and business is good. She is always interested in new ideas for things to sell.

She enjoys going out with her friends in the evening. She also loves tennis, but she doesn't often have time to play because she works very hard.

Marek Staniuk

Marek is Polish. He is twenty-six. When he finished school, he wanted to work in a different country. He worked in a textile factory in Amsterdam for four years. Some of the people he worked with were British, so he learnt to speak English and Dutch. He saved his money and when he went back to Poland, he bought a small gift shop. His uncle invested some money in the shop and helped Marek to set up a small import-export agency.

Marek wants to export Polish goods because he feels that there are a lot of unusual and beautiful craft products in Poland. He has no formal business qualifications, but he is very energetic and hard-working. He enjoys going out with his friends and he loves watching football.

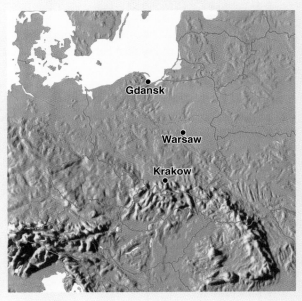

Reading

Read about this shop in London and answer the questions below.

In the photograph you can see an old shop in Highbury, London. It *belonged* to Giuseppe Volpe, a *relative* of Teresa and Peter. Giuseppe left Italy when he was a young man and went to live in London. He was a *tailor* who made and sold men's suits. The shop doesn't *look* very *promising* 有希望 at the moment, but it is in a very good position, right in the centre of the suburb of Highbury. Giuseppe stopped working two years ago, 市致 because he was *ill*.

Three weeks ago Giuseppe died suddenly. He had no children, but he loved young people. Before he died, he *left* the shop to Teresa and Peter, his two youngest *adult* relatives. They didn't know anything about their great-uncle Giuseppe's *will*. But yesterday they both had a *surprise* letter in their letterboxes.

1 Are these statements true or false? Explain why / why not.

  a Giuseppe Volpe's shop in London is now empty.

    _____

  b Giuseppe is a tailor.

    _____

  c Giuseppe was Peter and Teresa's grandfather.

    _____

  d Yesterday they had a surprise.

    _____

2 Match the words in *italics* with these definitions:

  a relation _____
  b was the property of _____
  c a legal document _____
  d unexpected _____
  e over the age of 18 _____
  f a person who makes clothes _____
  g appear _____
  h promised to give after his death _____
  i not well _____
  j showing signs of future success _____

Grammar
nouns, verbs, and adjectives

1 Look at these three sentences from the text:

It **belonged** to Giuseppe Volpe.
He was a **tailor**.
They both had a **surprise** letter.

– Which of the words in bold is a noun? … an adjective? … a verb?

– Say what these other words from the text are:

	noun	verb	adjective
relative	✓		
look	✓	✓	
promising			✓
ill	✓	✓	
left		✓	
adult	✓		
will		✓	

2 In which of these sentences is *surprise* used as a verb? … a noun? … an adjective?

a It was a lovely surprise to see you last week.
b Don't say anything to them. I want to surprise them.
c Peter had a surprise visit from a friend yesterday.

3 Complete the sentences below with one of these words. Use each word twice.

will   adult   tailor   look

a An _adult_ can open a bank account.
b After he died, no one found his _will_ .
c It doesn't _look_ very good.
d Our company offers _tailor_-made products to meet your needs.
e Some teenagers behave in an _adult_ way.
f The company _will_ pay you $1,000 for this idea.
g It can be really difficult to find a good _tailor_.
h I don't like the _look_ of this.

Listening

Read the list below.

Business is:

a being very busy   _S_
b taking risks   _M_
c working incredibly hard   ___
d organizing   ___
e making a good impression   _P_
f looking good   ___
g making a lot of money   ___
h being polite and efficient   ___
i going out to lunches   ___
j travelling a lot   ___
k solving problems   _T_
l meeting new people   ___
m being lucky   ___
n having fun   ___
o being stressed   ___

1 Listen to these people talking about business. Write *M* (for Marek); *T* (Teresa); *S* (Silvia); and *P* (Peter) next to their ideas in the list above.

2 What do you think is important? Can you add some ideas?

For me … is important.

1B Letter layout

Reading

1 Read this letter. Who do you think Frank Harrison is? What new information does he give?

① 20 HIGH STREET
HIGHBURY
LONDON N5
ENGLAND

② 2 October 2000

compliment
v.b 赞美 夸奖
take sth as a compliment

③ Peter Clapton
23 Greystone Street
Melbourne
Victoria
Australia

④ Dear Mr Clapton,

I regret to inform you that your great-uncle, Giuseppe Volpe, died in London, England, on 25 July this year.

⑤ He left you some property in his will. The property is to be divided between you and your cousin, Teresa Volpe, who lives in L'Aquila, Italy. The property consists of a shop in Highbury in north London and the sum of £10,000 each.

I would be grateful if you would contact me as soon as possible with your instructions. 指今

⑥ Yours sincerely,

⑦ *Frank Harrison*

Frank Harrison

2 What would you do with the shop?
I would sell it.
I would keep it.

3 Look at these names for different parts of a letter. Find examples of them in the letter.

a salutation ___4___ 问候
b signature ___7___
c date ___2___
d receiver's address ___3___
e complimentary close ___6___ 的免费赠送以软佩的3
f body of the letter ___5___
g letterhead / sender's address ___1___

Grammar
prepositions

1 Look at these sentences:

*I hope to come **to** Europe soon.*
*The letterhead is **at** the top of the page.*
*He died **in** London.*

— **Which of the words in bold describe movement?** *to*

— **Which describe position?** *at, in*

2 Complete these sentences with *at*, *in*, or *to*.

a I want to go __to__ England by plane.
b Do you live __in__ the centre?
c You put the signature after 'Yours sincerely', __at__ the bottom of the page.
d When can you come __to__ London, to talk about everything?
e He's not __at__ his desk at the moment.
f She is __in__ a meeting.

3 Describe the position of the different parts in the letter using these words:

at the top / bottom	in the centre
on the right / left	below the …
near the bottom left	above the …

EXAMPLE
The sender's address is on the right.

▶ **prepositions of movement and place** page 118

Listening

1 Here are some comments about running a shop.

  a Which are negative? Which are positive?

  1 Running a shop is very hard work.
  2 You can make a lot of money.
  3 You are your own boss.
  4 The hours are very long.
  5 You can meet a lot of people.
  6 There are big financial risks.
  7 There are a lot of interesting things to think about.
  8 You need to be a legal expert.

  b Can you add any more?

2   Now listen to a conversation in Peter's house in Australia. What is Peter's reaction to the letter from the lawyer?

MUM	… a shop in London! If you sell it, Peter, there'll be enough money for you to travel around Europe and …
PETER	Sell it! You must be joking. No, Mum. This is it! This is my big opportunity! A shop in England. I can open a new shop. I can see it now – 'Pete's Emporium'. I can import things from Australia. Sell the shop! No chance. I want to make a go of it.
MUM	It's not a bad idea, Peter. But what about your cousin? Perhaps she wants to sell it.
PETER	I can call her.
MUM	And Peter, it's very hard work, you know, running a shop. The hours are very long.
PETER	Mum, I like hard work. And this is just the beginning, you know. A little shop in London, then a group of shops in Britain, then a chain of shops all around the world. Rome, London, Paris, New York, Tokyo, Sydney … I can be a millionaire if I do this right.
MUM	Don't be silly, Peter. Get real! It's a big financial risk. You don't know what you're doing!
PETER	Why not, Mum? Millionaires always start with a simple idea.

3 Listen again.

  a Which points in **1** does Peter mention? Which does his mum mention?
  b What does Peter want to do with the shop?
  c What is his ambition? *To be …*
  d Do you think Teresa will agree with him?

Writing

This is Peter's reply to the lawyer, but the parts of it are mixed up.

1 Unscramble the letter.

  a I hope to come to Europe soon and discuss everything with her. After that I will be in a position to give you instructions.

  b Thank you for your letter of 2 October. Unfortunately, I can't give you instructions about the property immediately. I want to speak to my cousin Teresa first and give her time to think about the situation.

  c Dear Mr Harrison,

  d 20 October 2000

  e Peter Clapton

  f 23 Greystone Street
    Melbourne
    Victoria
    Australia

  g Yours sincerely,

2 Write it in the same format as the lawyer's letter.

1C Peter phones Teresa

Listening

Peter phones Teresa to talk about the shop.

1 ▭ Listen. Does Teresa want to keep the shop?

TERESA Well, I don't know! What do you think we should sell?

PETER We could sell gifts – you know, little presents and things like that.

TERESA But there are lots of gift shops in London already. I really don't think they need another gift shop.

PETER Yes, but Teresa, think! We could sell different things – things from Australia, things from Italy. There must be a market for original and unusual things.

TERESA What about capital? We'll need a lot of capital.

PETER No, don't forget that Giuseppe left us some money.

TERESA Yes, but I wanted to use that money for a holiday.

PETER Yes, I can understand your feelings, Teresa. But I think we should use the money for the future. I'd like to keep the shop.

TERESA Why don't you come to L'Aquila and we can discuss it?

PETER That's a good idea. Then we could both go to London to meet the lawyer and see the shop before we decide what to do.

2 Listen again. Which three of the points below do they discuss?

a what to sell in the shop
b what name to give the shop
c where to get capital
d where to get information
e how to advertise the shop
f what to do next

3 You and a partner want to open a shop.

a Look at the above list. With your partner think of as many ideas as you can for each point. This is a business technique called *brainstorming*.

USEFUL LANGUAGE
We could call it …
Why don't we sell …?
What about capital?
And information?
How about advertising?
That's a good idea.
I think we should sell …
Why not get capital from …?
We can ask …?
We could advertise it on radio / in a local paper.

b Tell other students about your ideas.

Speaking

1 🔊 Listen to parts of four phone conversations. In which one does the caller:

  a ask to speak to someone about a money problem?
  b leave a message?
  c ask to speak to Teresa?
  d apologize for a mistake?

2 Listen again. In each conversation what expression does the caller use when he / she asks to speak to someone?

3 In which conversation are these expressions used:

  a It's Peter, from Australia.
  b She's the person who deals with payments.
  c Can you tell him Maria called?
  d I think you have the wrong number.
  e Speaking.
  f Sorry to disturb you.

Pronunciation

1 🔊 Listen, and repeat these words with the correct stress.

mistake ●●   **wanted** ●●

2 🔊 Now put these words in the correct category, then listen and check.

disturb	payment	message	office	decide
number	address	speaking	idea	discuss

mistake ●●	**wanted** ●●
disturb	

Grammar
past simple

1 Look at these sentences:

  Giuseppe left us some money.
  The shop belonged to Giuseppe.

  – Underline the verb in each sentence.
  – Which one is regular? Which is irregular? How do we know the difference?

2 Which of these verbs have irregular past forms? What are they?

want	stop	die	have
love	feel	make	sell

3 Complete these sentences with the correct form of a verb from the list above.

  a I _____ to come to see you yesterday, but I _____ ill.
  b On the way to his meeting, he _____ at a phone box and _____ a call.
  c Last year the company _____ more products than the year before.
  d Great-uncle Giuseppe _____ last year.
  e She _____ the film, but he hated it.
  f I _____ lunch with my boss yesterday.

▶ **past simple** page 118
▶ **irregular verbs** page 122

2A Places

Reading

1 In L'Aquila, Teresa and Peter are preparing for their visit to London. They write a list of things they have to do. Complete the list with these verbs:

> Find   Arrange   Book   Find out

a _____ about London and Highbury.
b _____ tickets.
c _____ a meeting with the lawyer.
d _____ accommodation.

2 Now they are looking at some commercial information about London. Separate the information into the four categories below. Write the category number next to each piece of information.

1 population
2 geography
3 transport and communications
4 industries and employment

a London is situated on the River Thames in the south-east of England.   *2*
b Paper, printing, and publishing are the main manufacturing industries.   _____
c Almost half of London homes have single occupants.   _____
d The London area has the highest number of different ethnic groups in the UK.   _____
e London is one of the world's major tourist destinations and there are over 200,000 people who work in tourism.   _____
f The population of London was 15,000 in 1100; today it is over 7 million.   _____
g London is now linked by rail to many major European cities.   _____
h There are around 30,000 retail establishments with over 300,000 employees.   _____
i Other important industries include electrical and electronic engineering, food, drink, tobacco, chemicals, and man-made fibres.   _____
j London has five international airports.   _____
k The City of London, which employs over 700,000 people, is an important financial centre.   _____

3 Match the words in columns **A** and **B**.

A	B
financial	engineering
man-made	centre
international	fibres
electronic	industry
manufacturing	airports

4 Describe your home town.

5 🔊 Listen to Peter and Teresa talking about L'Aquila and London.

a Which of the items in the list below does Peter mention?
b Which does Teresa mention?

medieval buildings _____   black taxis _____
red buses _____   safe streets _____
music shops _____   town centre _____
green parks _____   shop windows _____
city streets _____   night clubs _____
hamburger bars _____

Grammar
noun + noun expressions

1 Look at these sentences:

I remember **music** *shops.*
I like **good** *music.*

– Which words tell us more about the nouns?

– Which of these words is also a noun?

In noun + noun expressions, the first noun acts as an adjective.

2 Find the other examples of noun + noun expressions (where nouns describe other nouns) in the list in **5** opposite.

3 Make five more noun + noun expressions with these words. Use each word once only.

EXAMPLE
telephone directory

~~telephone~~	fax	ticket	~~directory~~
ink	computer	shop	clothes
pen	train	machine	screen

Speaking

Look at these notes about numbers:

– A number of hundreds or thousands is singular:
  600: six hundre̱d
  5,000: five thousaṉd

– In British English we use *and* between hundreds and tens, and between thousands and tens:
  935: nine hundred and thirty-five
  2,023: two thousand and twenty-three

– A percentage is spoken like this:
  22.65%: twenty-two point six five per cent

– In writing, a comma indicates thousands:
  6,569: six thousand five hundred and sixty-nine

▶ **numbers** page 117

1 🔊 Listen and write down the numbers and percentages you hear.

a _____ e _____

b _____ f _____

c _____ g _____

d _____ h _____

2 Peter and Teresa need information about Highbury. Look at the pie chart about the local population.

  a How many people are between the ages of 25 and 34?
  b What percentage of the local population is that?

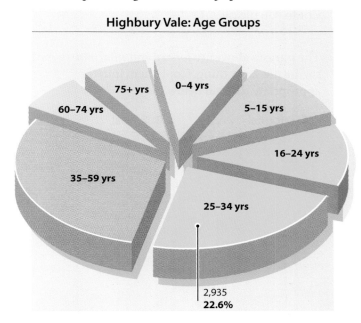

Highbury Vale: Age Groups

75+ yrs · 0–4 yrs · 60–74 yrs · 5–15 yrs · 16–24 yrs · 35–59 yrs · 25–34 yrs

2,935
22.6%

3 In pairs, complete the chart by asking about the other age groups.

Student A
Use File 1 on page 86 to ask about some of the age groups. Then answer Student B's questions.

Student B
Use File 22 on page 92 to answer Student A's questions. Then ask about some of the age groups.

4 Do those statistics suggest Highbury is a good place to sell:

  – jeans?
  – DJ equipment?
  – gifts?

2B Formality and informality

Reading

1 Draw a line to link the expressions that have the same functions.

Dear Sir / Madam,   I am writing about …

Best regards,   Can you …?

I am writing with   Dear Mr Warton,
reference to …
                                     (I look forward to) your
(I look forward to)   early reply.
hearing from you soon.
                                     Yours faithfully,
I enclose …
                                     Dear John,
Yours sincerely,
                                     Please find enclosed …
Could you please …?

2 The phrases above are *formal* and *informal* ways of saying the same thing. Copy them into the appropriate column below.

A informal	**B** formal

3 Complete the following formal letter using some of the expressions above.

> Dear ¹_____ ,
>
> ²_____ your advertisement in the Office Times on 13 July.
>
> ³_____ send me further details as I am interested in buying office furniture for my company. ⁴_____ a list of our requirements.
>
> I look forward to ⁵_____ .
>
> ⁶_____ ,

Writing

Simple phrases like these can be used in all kinds of business letters. Below are some more examples.

Use them to complete this letter to a friend of Peter's mother.

a I enclose a …
b We are really looking forward to …
c Can you send us …?
d You asked about …
e It is very kind of you …
f We'll let you know …

> Dear Mrs Bolton,
>
> Thank you very much for your postcard. We are coming to London one day next week.
>
> ¹_____ our plans: I hope to open Giuseppe's shop again. I really want to make a go of it but Teresa is not sure. We would like to look at it carefully first before we decide what to do.
>
> ²_____ to offer us a place to stay. We'd love to accept your invitation, at least for a week or two until we find our way around.
>
> ³_____ our travel plans but please don't come and meet us at the airport. I'm sure we can find our own way to your house. ⁴_____ instructions for how to get there and a map?
>
> ⁵_____ recent photograph of Mum and the family. She sends her love and says she would love to see you again. She is well and busy – as usual!!
>
> Thank you again for your kind offer of hospitality.
>
> ⁶_____ meeting you.
>
> Best regards,
>
> *Peter*

Grammar
infinitive with and without *to*

1 Look at these sentences:

*I **want** to make a go of the shop.*
*We **can** find our own way.*

– Which of the verbs in bold italics is followed by an infinitive without *to*? … by an infinitive with *to*?

2 Which of these verbs can be followed by an infinitive without *to*?

could	would like	would love
decide	should	hope

3 Complete the sentences below with the correct form of the verb in brackets.

EXAMPLE
I can (see) it now: 'Sports Video Specialists'.
*I can **see** it now: 'Sports Video Specialists'.*

a We could (start) a new company.
b I think we should (open) a new branch.
c They want (go) to Spain.
d I need (speak) to my colleague.
e You must (be) joking.
f I can't (help) you this week.
g I'd love (live) abroad.
h I'd like (talk) to you about next year's budget.

4 Complete Mrs Bolton's reply to Peter's letter using the words in the box. Sometimes you will need to use *to*.

get off	see	know
meet	hear	stay

Thank you for your letter. I'm glad you have decided ¹____ with us. I enclose a map of the area near my house. You should ²____ the underground at the Angel and follow the roads marked in yellow.

Thank you for the photo of your mother. I'd really like ³____ her again, too.

Let me ⁴____ the exact time of your arrival. My daughter works at the airport so she could ⁵____ you there!

I hope ⁶____ from you soon.

▶ **verb + infinitive with and without *to*** page 122

Dictation

1 🔊 Listen to Teresa as she writes a letter to Mrs Bolton. What present is mentioned?

2 Listen again and write down the letter.

3 Write a letter to a friend to thank him / her for an invitation to dinner.

2C Travel arrangements

Listening

Peter and Teresa have a problem with their flight to London.

1 ▭ Listen to Peter talking to Mrs Bolton about their new travel arrangements. What is the new flight number?

2 Listen again.

   a What day is the new flight?
   b What date is the new flight?
   c What is the time of their arrival (local time)?

3 Now read the conversation in pairs.

MRS BOLTON Hello?
PETER Hello. Can I speak to Mrs Bolton, please?
MRS BOLTON Speaking.
PETER This is Peter Clapton calling from Italy. How are you, Mrs Bolton?
MRS BOLTON I'm fine, thanks. And you? Are you excited about coming to London?
PETER Yeah, and I'm very excited about seeing the shop. Actually, I'm phoning to say that our flight has been changed. We're coming on a different flight.
MRS BOLTON I'm sorry, I didn't catch that.
PETER I said we're coming on a different flight. We're now coming on the next day, on Friday the eighteenth. Our new flight number is AZ 564. We're arriving at two o'clock in the afternoon your time.
MRS BOLTON So, that's Friday the eighteenth and your flight number is AZ 564. You're arriving at two o'clock in the afternoon our time.
PETER That's right. Is that a problem for you?
MRS BOLTON No, that's fine. See you soon.

4 What does Mrs Bolton say when she wants Peter to repeat something?

Grammar
future arrangements

1 Look at these two sentences:

I'm phoning to say that our new flight number is AZ 564.

We're coming on a different flight.

– Which of these sentences refers to the present?

– Which refers to the future?

2 The form *I'm / We're + -ing* is often used to refer to a future arrangement. Find other examples in the telephone conversation.

3 Now talk about the flights in this two-week European tour:

EXAMPLE
We are leaving London on the first of February at ten past nine and arriving in Brussels at eleven twenty …

From	Date	Depart	To	Arrive
London	1 Feb.	0910	Brussels	1120
Brussels	2 Feb.	1000	Prague	1125
Prague	3 Feb.	0900	Munich	1015
Munich	5 Feb.	1130	Istanbul	1505
Istanbul	7 Feb.	1535	Florence via Rome	2205
Florence	10 Feb.	1325	Seville via Barcelona	1755
Seville	12 Feb.	1440	Lisbon via Madrid	1655
Lisbon	14 Feb.	1805	London	2045

▶ **future** page 114
▶ **time** page 121

Speaking

Pronunciation

Many common words, like *am*, *are*, *is*, *has*, *have*, are often contracted when we speak. For example, we don't say:
/æm/   I <u>am</u> coming on the 18th.

We say:
/m/   I'<u>m</u> coming on the 18th.

1 ▭ Listen to these sentences and underline the words that are contracted in spoken English.

EXAMPLE
<u>I am</u> coming on a different flight.

a My flight has been changed.
b He is coming on a different flight.
c I would like to see you tomorrow.
d I have finished.
e They are arriving at three o'clock.

2 Practise repeating the sentences using the contracted forms.

3 What are the full forms of the contracted verbs below?

EXAMPLE
You're late.
You are late.

a They're coming by car. ____
b We've a long day tomorrow. ____
c She'd like to meet you. ____
d He's in Turkey at the moment. ____
e He's got a meeting this morning. ____

Role-play

1 In pairs, role-play other changes to flights.

Student A
Phone Student B.
See File 2 on page 86 for information.

Student B
Answer the phone.
See File 23 on page 92 for information.

USEFUL LANGUAGE
Speak slowly, please.
I'm afraid I can't speak English very well.
Sorry, could you repeat that, please?
I'm sorry, I didn't catch that.
I'm arriving at …

2 Change roles.

Student A
Answer the phone.
See File 3 on page 86 for new information.

Student B
Phone Student A.
See File 24 on page 92 for new information.

3A The shop

Listening

Teresa and Peter visit the shop.

1 Study the plan.

EXAMPLE
Is the front room smaller than the back room?
No, it isn't.

a Is there a toilet? _____
b Is there a doorway between the front room and the back room? _____
c Is there enough room for a storeroom? _____
d Is there enough light for a shop? _____
e Is it suitable for a gift shop? _____

2 Teresa and Peter are measuring the shop. Complete the conversation with the words in the box below.

height	wide	measurements
high	long	length

PETER	Let's take the ¹ _____. Have you got a tape measure?
TERESA	Yes, I have.
PETER	Okay, let's start with the walls. How ² _____ is this wall?
TERESA	Hold the end of the tape measure. Let me see, that's five metres and fifty centimetres.
PETER	Did you say fifty or fifteen?
TERESA	Fifty, five oh.
PETER	Okay, so that's ³ _____ – five metres fifty. Now let's measure the height.
TERESA	Okay, but I need a chair to stand on.
PETER	Can you read it now? How ⁴ _____ is it?
TERESA	Three metres twenty.
PETER	⁵ _____ – three metres twenty. Let's do the width of the door now.
TERESA	Just a minute, let's see … that's one metre ten ⁶ _____.
PETER	So that's …

3 🔲 Now listen and check your answers.

4 Continue Peter and Teresa's conversation as they measure the other walls, the doors, and windows.

USEFUL LANGUAGE
How high is the back room?
What's the length of the side wall?
How wide is this window?
What's the width of this door?

▶ **measurements** page 115

Speaking

Teresa falls in love with London and she wants to keep the shop.

1 Brainstorm names for the shop.

2 Unscramble these words to find the name Peter and Teresa choose for the shop:

TREENPS   MEIT

3 They imagine the shop with new furniture and colours. Separate these colours:

redblackpinkdarkyellowpurplelightbluepalegreenorange

4 Which colours would *you* use in a gift shop?

5 Look at the items of furniture below. Match the items to the pictures. Which do you really need in a shop?

table	chair
umbrella stand	display shelves
stereo	cupboard
sofa	coffee table

a b c
d e
f g h

Grammar
have and *have got*

1 Look at these sentences:

Do you have size A?
*Yes, we **do**. / No, we **don't**.*

Have you got size A?
*Yes, we **have**. / No, we **haven't**.*

– The verb is different. Is the meaning the same?

2 Now answer these questions:

EXAMPLE
Do you have a car? *No, I don't.*
Have you got a brother? *Yes, I have.*

a Have you got any white shelves?
b Does she have a good job?
c Has he got a big office?
d Have they got time to wait?
e Do we have the right address?

▶ **present simple** page 119

Role-play

1 In pairs, role-play conversations in furniture shops.

Student A
Look at File 4 on page 86.

Student B
Look at File 25 on page 92.

USEFUL LANGUAGE
I'm looking for some …   *What size do you need?*
display shelves   *What sizes do you have?*
cupboards   *How much do they cost?*
glass   *I'll have two of those.*

▶ **countable and uncountable nouns** page 113

2 Now change roles.
Student A
Look at File 5 on page 86.

Student B
Look at File 26 on page 92.

3B Good commercial letters

Reading

In business, good letters must be well-organized, clear, and polite.

1 Complete the hints below for writing good commercial letters with these verbs.

Use   Explain   Exclude   Be   Put

a _____ what a letter is about in the first sentence of the first paragraph.
b _____ simple but precise language.
c _____ only one main idea in a paragraph.
d _____ all irrelevant information.
e _____ polite.

2 A good letter communicates ideas clearly and memorably. Which version of this letter (A or B) is more memorable?

3 Do the two versions opposite follow the hints in **1a–e**?

Grammar
order of adjectives

1 Look at this noun phrase:

two small green leather bags

The headword is *bags*. In what order are the following adjectives given: colour, size, material, number?

2 Put the words below in the right order.

a big three bottles plastic blue
b yellow bands rubber large ten
c paper pink enormous four hats
d black little boxes metal six

▸ **order of adjectives** page 117

▸ order of adjectives page 117

A

Dear Mr Jenkins,

I don't like the files you sent us this morning. They were the wrong ones. They weren't plastic and they weren't grey, like the ones we ordered on 9 June. And they weren't the right size. They were a horrible bright pink. We wanted A4 files, not A5. I tried one out. My papers did not fit. My colleague has some smart large grey plastic files. She bought them from you. That's why we ordered the same ones.

Yours sincerely,

Jeff Short

B

Dear Mr Jenkins,

I am writing to say that the files you sent us this morning were the wrong size and colour, pink A5 instead of grey A4.

Please could you send us replacements as soon as possible: 15 grey A4 files, as ordered on 9 June.

Yours sincerely,

Jeff Short

Writing

Peter wants information about Australian things they could sell in a gift shop.

1 Read his first draft opposite and cross out anything that is irrelevant.

2 Now copy out the new version in two paragraphs.

Begin paragraph 1:
My cousin and I are planning to …

Begin paragraph 2:
Can you please send us …

3 Complete the first paragraphs of some different commercial letters with the words below.

inform	apologize	invite
thank	complain	confirm

a We would like to _____ you to a small party to celebrate the opening of our shop.
b We are writing to _____ for sending you the wrong order.
c I am writing to _____ about the poor quality of the goods that we received today.
d This letter is to _____ your reservation for a single room on 22nd March.
e I am writing to _____ you that your order is ready for collection.
f I am writing to _____ you for the useful information that you sent me.

Dictation

Monica Taylor has received a wrong order from her supplier, Mr Jordan. She dictates a reply to her secretary.

1 🔊 Listen. In the letter, which of the following does she refer to:

– hats?
– cats?
– caps?
– bats?

2 What size does she want? When were they ordered?

3 Listen again and write down the letter.

Dear Sir / Madam,

My cousin Teresa Volpe and I are planning to open a shop in London. It is still in a terrible mess. We have to clean it and paint it. We would like to sell Australian and Italian products. We think this is a good idea because Teresa is from Italy and I'm from Australia. Can you please send us a list of suppliers for Australian products, including:

– things like boomerangs
– T-shirts and clothes with aboriginal patterns (I have got a T-shirt like this and I really love it!)
– any other ideas?

It is very difficult to know who to contact so we would be very happy if you could help. We are also interested in having more information about the following:

– How about trade fairs? We don't know where they are.
– I also think magazines that advertise Australian products might be a good place to look for information.

Thank you for your assistance.

Yours faithfully,

Peter Clapton

3C Getting through

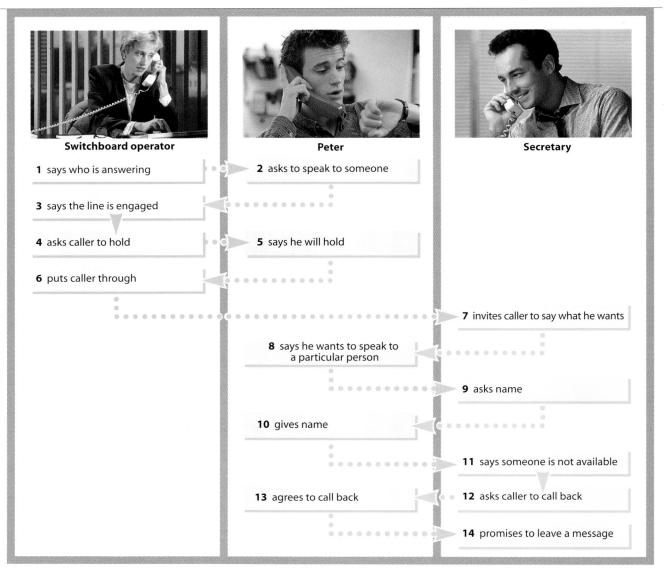

Switchboard operator

1 says who is answering

3 says the line is engaged

4 asks caller to hold

6 puts caller through

Peter

2 asks to speak to someone

5 says he will hold

8 says he wants to speak to a particular person

10 gives name

13 agrees to call back

Secretary

7 invites caller to say what he wants

9 asks name

11 says someone is not available

12 asks caller to call back

14 promises to leave a message

Listening

Peter wants to speak to the Trade Commissioner at the Australian High Commission in London.

1 [cassette] Listen. Does he get through?

2 Look at the stages of the conversation.

3 Listen again, and match the phrases below to the correct stage above.

a Who's calling, please? _____9_____
b Yes, I'll hold. _____
c I'd like to speak to the Trade Commissioner, please. _____
d Good morning. Australian High Commission. _____

e I'm afraid the Trade Commissioner is in a meeting at the moment. _____
f Will you hold? _____
g My name is Peter Clapton. _____
h Okay, I'll call back at about four o'clock. _____
i The line's free now. I'm putting you through. _____
j Can you call back this afternoon? _____
k Goodbye. I'll tell him you called. _____
l Trade Commissioner's office. How can I help you? _____
m I'm afraid the line's engaged. _____
n I'd like to speak to Mr Cody, please. _____

4 Now use the flow chart to practise the conversation.

Grammar

expressions with *will*

1 Look at these sentences:

I'll call back about four o' clock.
I'll tell him you called.

– What time is Peter going to call back? When does he make that decision?

– The form *'ll* + infinitive is used in spoken English when we decide now to do something.

2 Match situations **a–d** with sentences **1–4** below.

  a The phone rings.
  b A client needs a document.
  c A friend has a big problem.
  d A colleague's printer isn't working.

  1 I'll print it for you.
  2 I'll help you.
  3 I'll get it.
  4 I'll send it immediately.

▶ **future** page 114

Pronunciation

In questions, the voice can go up or down at the end.

1 📼 Listen. Does the speaker's voice go up or down? Write ↑ or ↓ after each question, like this:

EXAMPLE
Are you busy? ↑

  a What's your name? _____
  b Will you hold? _____
  c Who's calling please? _____
  d Is he free next week? _____
  e Will you call back later? _____
  f Are you free next week? _____
  g When are you free? _____
  h How can I help you? _____
  i What would you like to know? _____

2 Can you answer *Yes* or *No* to any of the questions? What is the rule for intonation in:

  a *Yes* / *No* questions?
  b *Wh-* questions?

3 Listen again, and repeat the questions with the correct intonation.

Speaking

Role-play

1 In pairs, role-play telephone conversations like the one on the opposite page. Use the information in the table.

Student A
You are the caller. Ask to speak to these people.

Student B
You are the operator and the secretary. Give reasons why they are not available.

2 Now change roles.

Name	Mr Singh Ms Wood Miss Ashton Mrs Miller
Job	Marketing Manager at UBI Toys Advertising Executive at London News Manager of London Tourist Office Head of the Delivery Department at Ossie Clothes
Reasons why they are not available	in a meeting out of the office right now on holiday at lunch
Times to call back	tomorrow next week in an hour this afternoon

She's not in the office at the moment.

4A At a trade fair

Speaking

Teresa and Peter go to a trade fair to look for ideas for the shop.

1 In which of these halls will they find the products below?

a Art
b Leather Goods
c Stationery

paints	greeting cards	wallets
frames	pens	diaries
briefcases	leather jackets	wrapping paper
posters	prints	luggage

2 At one of the stands Peter and Teresa *fill in* a market research questionnaire. Fill in your own answers to the questionnaire. Part One is on a scale of 1–3 (1 = always; 2 = sometimes; 3 = never).

▶ **adverbs of frequency** page 112

	▼ Peter	▼ Teresa	▼ You	▼ Your partner
Part One				
1 Is fashion important to you?	3	1		
2 Do you look at labels?	3	1		
3 Is quality important to you?	2	1		
4 Do you spend more than £10 on birthday presents?	2	1		
5 Do you choose special or unusual gifts for friends?	1	2		
Part Two				
6 What are the last three things you bought as gifts?	boomerang, CD, poster	photograph frame, china, pen		
7 What are the last three things you bought for yourself?	leather jacket, designer pen, wallet	rug, picture, alarm clock		

3 In pairs, ask your partner about his / her ideas and fill in the last column of the table.

4 Can you think of some more questions to add?

▼ Three-dimensional T-shirts
Price each: _____
Price for ten: _____

4A

Listening

Peter and Teresa visit three stands selling T-shirts.

1 🔲 Listen to three conversations and match them to the pictures.

2 Listen again.
   a How much is each T-shirt?
   b What is the price for ten?

► Philosophy Football T-shirts
Price each: _____
Price for ten: _____

▲ Tourist T-shirts
Price each: _____
Price for ten: _____

Grammar
comparatives and superlatives

1 Look at these sentences comparing the prices of T-shirts:

   *The tourist T-shirts are **cheaper** than the three-dimensional ones.*

   *Philosophy Football T-shirts are **more expensive** than the tourist T-shirts.*

   When do we use adjective + -er? … more + adjective?

2 Read and underline the words used to compare prices and profitability.

   Green hats cost £2.50. They are <u>cheaper than</u> red hats which cost £3.00. Blue hats are the cheapest at £1.99 each. If you sell all the hats at £5.00 each, the most profitable are the blue ones and the least profitable are the red ones. Green hats are more profitable than red ones and less profitable than blue ones.

3 Write a similar paragraph comparing the prices and profitability of T-shirts using the information in the table.

Item	Cost Price	Selling Price	Profit
Skateboard Design	£12.50	£15.00	£2.50
Football Team	£17.00	£23.00	£6.00
Famous Faces	£3.00	£7.99	£4.99

► **comparatives and superlatives** page 112

4B A letter of enquiry

Reading

1 Match these explanations with one of the noun phrases in the advertisement:

a a free example of a T-shirt
b very good T-shirts
c you don't pay for the design
d you must order 20 T-shirts or more
e you can receive the T-shirts anywhere in the world

① SWEATSHIRTS AND T-SHIRTS
printed to your own design
(min. order 20)

Free Design Service
High Quality Shirts
Free Proof Garment
Fast, Efficient Service

Tel: 01483 555612
UK / WORLDWIDE DELIVERY

For a pack with FREE full colour information contact:
Classic T-shirts, Gilbert House, Guildford Trading Estate, GU3 7EX

2 A letter of enquiry is usually in two paragraphs. Read this letter, then complete the column in the table for Advert 1.

Dear Sir / Madam,

We are a large discotheque in the centre of London. We are organizing a new series of dance competitions and are thinking of giving away specially designed T-shirts as prizes. I saw your advertisement for T-shirts in last week's *Discoworld* and am interested in knowing more about your service.

Could you please send us a free full colour information pack as soon as possible?

Yours faithfully,

James Silvers

James Silvers

Dictation

Teresa is dictating a letter for Peter to send to the wig shop Hair Raisers.

1 As you listen:

a underline the name of the magazine she mentions.
  – The Race   – Rates
  – The Face   – Fame

	Advert 1	Advert 2
In paragraph one: say who you are and why you're writing **and / or** say how you heard about the company / person	We ¹___ a large … We ²___ ___ a new … and ³___ of giving … I ⁴___ your advertisement … and ⁵___ interested in …	
In paragraph two: make a specific request or enquiry	⁶___ you ⁷___ send us …	

b correct the address of Hair Raisers.

1–14 Staincross House
Broad Street
London NW7

c say when Teresa is opening the shop.
– soon
– shortly
– as soon as possible
– on Saturday

2 Listen again and write the letter down.

3 Complete the last column of the table with expressions from the dictation.

Grammar
present continuous

1 Look at these sentences:

*Our company **makes** wigs for musicals.*
*We **are making** wigs for a production of the musical 'Hair'.*

– **Which sentence refers to something that the company does all the time?**

2 **For each of the services below write a sentence saying what they are working on at the moment.**

EXAMPLE
We do market research for shops.
(new music shop)

At present we are doing market research for a new music shop.

a We run advertising campaigns for new businesses. (a new record shop)
b We organize big society events. (a big dance)
c We make wooden furniture. (desks)
d We design hotel kitchens. (a kitchen for a new hotel in Paris)

▶ **present continuous** page 118
▶ **present simple** page 119

Writing

Look at the advertisement. Write and ask for a complete illustrated catalogue and current price list. Write two paragraphs.

Cards, Cards, Cards!
Birthdays · Weddings · Good luck
Congratulations

… only a small part of our list. Give your customers the best choice in town with our unique range of greeting cards.

For further information write to: X-pressions, Unit 15, Hill Trading Estate, London N12 7EL, or fax 0181-217-2301

USEFUL LANGUAGE
I was given your name by …
I saw your advertisement in …
We … (say what your company does)
At the moment we are …
Could you please send us …?
Would you kindly send us …?
Please can you let me have …?
Yours faithfully,

4C Messages

Listening

1 🔊 Listen to three answerphone messages in a stationer's shop and write down the names (1 and 2).

a MESSAGE

Please send Mr ¹_____ of ²_____ Community School the following items:

³_____ staplers

⁴_____ pairs of scissors

b MESSAGE

Please send Mrs ¹_____ of ²_____ Enterprises PLC these articles:

³_____ files

⁴_____ packets of paper clips

c MESSAGE

Please send Jean ¹_____ from ²_____ Consultancies Ltd. the following:

³_____ rubbers

⁴_____ blue Biros

2 Listen again and write down the numbers (3 and 4).

3 Understanding spelling on the phone can be difficult. Sometimes this international aviation system is used:

A	Alpha	N	November
B	Bravo	O	Oscar
C	Charlie	P	Papa
D	Delta	Q	Quebec
E	Echo	R	Romeo
F	Foxtrot	S	Sierra
G	Golf	T	Tango
H	Hotel	U	Uniform
I	India	V	Victor
J	Juliette	W	Whisky
K	Kilo	X	X-ray
L	Lima	Y	Yankee
M	Mike	Z	Zulu

What system is used in your country?

4 Practise spelling the following names, like this:

A for Alpha (British English)

or

A as in Alpha (American English)

- Luciana   - Dominik   - Esperanza
- Jâcques   - Xavier   - Wolfgang
- Yveline   - Mehmet   - Bora

Pronunciation

1 Which other letters of the alphabet have the same vowel sounds as these:

/eɪ/	/iː/	/e/	/aɪ/	/əʊ/	/uː/	/ɑː/
a	b	f	i	o	q	r

2 🔊 Look at the following words in phonetic script and say them. Listen and check.

a /meɪk/ _____   **h** /baɪ/ _____

b /peɪpə/ _____   **i** /fəʊn/ _____

c /kiːp/ _____   **j** /gəʊ/ _____

d /friː/ _____   **k** /njuː/ _____

e /jes/ _____   **l** /truː/ _____

f /leðə/ _____   **m** /stɑːf/ _____

g /faɪlz/ _____   **n** /ɑːsk/ _____

3 Now spell them.

4 Complete these words with the correct vowel sound from **1**.

a screen   /skr__n/

b staple   /st__pəl/

c computer   /kəmpj__tə/

d poster   /p__stə/

e through   /θr__/

f prices   /pr__səz/

g cheap   /tʃ__p/

h car   /k__/

i then   /ð__n/

j soon   /s__n/

Eastnor Pottery
CONTEMPORARY CERAMICS

Clock Cottage
Home Farm
Eastnor
Ledbury
Herefordshire
HR8 1RD

Telephone|Fax
01531 633255

First order would be proforma.

With compliments

Speaking

1 In pairs, practise spelling and copying down names and numbers.

Student A
See File 6 on page 87.

Student B
Copy down the names and numbers your partner tells you.

2 Change roles.

Student A
Copy down the names and numbers your partner tells you.

Student B
See File 27 on page 93.

USEFUL LANGUAGE
How do you spell that?
Could you repeat that please?
Sorry, how many did you say?
Sorry, I didn't catch that.

3 Peter gets this note in reply to a letter of enquiry: *First order would be proforma.* What does *proforma* mean? To find out, read the entries below and answer these questions:

a What is a *proforma invoice?*
b How do you pronounce *invoice?* And *proforma?*
c Is *invoice* a noun or a verb?
d What does *to invoice* mean?
e What is the plural of *invoice?*
f What verbs are often used before the noun *invoice?*
g What words are often used after the verb *invoice?*

invoice¹ *noun* (commerce) a list of goods sold or services received that states how much you must pay for them: *We haven't received payment for our invoice dated 3 September.*	/ˈɪnvɔɪs / **pl** invoices ◄ pay, receive, send (out) an **invoice** ► **proforma invoice**
invoice² *verb* (commerce) **1** to make a list of goods sold or services received with their prices **2** to send a list of goods sold or services received as a request for payment: *Please invoice me for the goods.*	/ˈɪnvɔɪs / **invoice, invoicing, invoiced** **note** transitive verb ◄ **invoice** someone *for* something; **invoice** someone *on* (a certain date)
proforma invoice *noun* (commerce) an invoice that is sent in advance of goods supplied: *send a proforma invoice to a new customer*	/prəʊˌfɔːməˈɪnvɔɪs / **pl** proforma invoices ◄ enclose, send a **proforma invoice** ► **invoice¹**

Extracts from the *Oxford Dictionary of Business English for Learners of English*

5A Meeting new people

Listening

You are at a trade fair. You see someone who looks interesting.

1 What questions could you ask to get into conversation with her / him?

2 Which questions in this list are *inappropriate* to start a conversation?

a I'm sure I've seen you somewhere before.
b Have you been to many fairs?
c That's a really nice shirt you're wearing. Where did you get it?
d What do you think of the fair?
e Have you been in business long?
f Can I get you a drink? It's very hot in here!
g Are you here alone?
h I saw you this morning at the T-shirt stand. Did you order any?
i Have you found any interesting products here?
j Are you here to sell or to buy?

3 🔲 Listen to a conversation between Peter and Silvia. Which of the sentences above do they use?

4 🔲 Listen to Teresa talking to Marek. Which sentences do they use?

5 🔲 Listen to Peter introducing Silvia to Teresa. Fill in the missing words.

> PETER   Teresa, I'd like you <u>¹____</u> Silvia. She has a very successful gift shop in Barcelona.
> TERESA <u>²____</u> to meet you, Silvia.
> SILVIA <u>³____</u> to meet you.
> PETER   She has some fantastic ideas.

6 Role-play Teresa introducing Marek to Peter. Marek has got a little gift shop and small export agency in Gdańsk, and he's got some very interesting ideas about Polish products for export.

Grammar
present perfect with *ever* and *yet*

1 Look at these questions:

Have you seen the toy stands?
Have you been to this trade fair before?

Yes, I have.
No, I haven't.

– Which question asks what you have done today? … in your whole life?

– To which question can you add *ever*? … and *yet*?

2 Complete the questions below with one of these words:

> found   been   talked   met   worked   seen

EXAMPLE
*Have we **met** before?*

a Have you ____ any interesting products?
b Have you ____ the stationery hall?
c Have you ____ to any new suppliers?
d Have you ____ to Poland?
e Have you ____ in a big company?

3 Now add *ever* or *yet* to each sentence.

EXAMPLE
*Have we **ever** met before?*

▶ **present perfect** page 119

Role-play

In pairs, continue the conversations between Silvia and Teresa, and between Peter and Marek.

1 **Student A** You are Silvia. Look at File 7 on page 87.
Student B You are Teresa. Look at File 28 on page 93.

USEFUL LANGUAGE
Have you travelled a lot?
Have you ever been to America?
How do you feel about your work?
What did you do before that?
Why are you at the fair?
Which stands have you seen?

2 **Student A** You are Peter. Look at File 8 on page 87.
Student B You are Marek. Look at File 29 on page 93.

Reading

Read about Peter, Teresa, Marek, and Silvia. Answer the questions opposite.

Peter and Teresa are full partners – they share responsibility for management and they *take an equal share* of the profits and are both *liable* for any *losses*. They went to a lawyer to draw up a partnership agreement as they felt it was better to have everything written down in black and white.

Silvia is a sole trader and usually likes her independence, although she feels a bit insecure sometimes.

Marek and his uncle are partners but Marek's uncle is a *sleeping partner*. He doesn't help Marek to make decisions or manage the business but he has invested his capital. He is liable for losses and *debts* but, of course, he hopes to *make a profit*.

Peter, Teresa, Silvia, and Marek realize that as small businesses they have a lot of problems in common. They decide to form a group in order to get better discounts from suppliers; to help each other find original products to sell; and to learn from each other by benchmarking.

1 Which of the words in *italics* mean:

a amounts of money that you owe?
b to get back more money than you invest?
c legally responsible for a debt?
d to receive the same percentage of the profits?
e amounts of money that you lose?
f someone who invests in a company but doesn't make decisions?

2 Answer these questions:

a Does Peter earn more money from the shop than Teresa?
b What does Marek's uncle do in the management of the business?
c Who does Silvia share her profits with?
d Are they all liable for losses?
e What do they decide to do? Why?

3 The new partners prepare the informal agreement below to discuss with a lawyer. Complete it with these words:

promote	ideas	orders	e-mail
discounts	products	compare	

We the undersigned agree:

1. to place at least six _____ a year as a group to obtain better _____ .

2. to meet three times a year to decide what _____ to order.

3. to tell each other about new _____ and products.

4. to benchmark, i.e. provide information so that we can _____ performance and learn from each other.

5. to set up a system of easy communication between the members of the group using _____.

6. to _____ craft products from Poland, Italy, Spain, and Australia.

Reading

1 In a letter of reply to an enquiry, in what order do you:

   a say you are enclosing information?
   b invite further contact / enquiries?
   c thank the potential customer for the enquiry?
   d try to persuade the customer to do business?

2 Look at the letter of reply below. How many paragraphs are there? In which one (A, B, or C) does the writer do the above (**a–d**)?

3 Underline the expressions in paragraphs A and C which could be used in a reply to a request for information for any product or service.

4 Now look at the language used in paragraph B to *promote* Tees Total and complete the table below with suitable words / phrases.

Product	Service
Design:	Design of motif: *free of charge*
Shirts:	Proof garment: Delivery: Service: Guarantee:

TEES TOTAL
PRINTING AND
EMBROIDERY OF
LEISUREWEAR

HIGH STREET
WOOTON BASSETT
NR. SWINDON
WILTSHIRE
SN4 7AB
TEL (01793) 849888
FAX (01793) 849890

Teresa Volpe
12 High Street
Highbury
London N5

18 May 2000

Dear Ms Volpe,

(A) Thank you for your enquiry regarding the printing of T-shirts to your own design. Please find enclosed our latest information package, which we hope is of interest to you.

(B) We offer professional design of your motif free of charge, a free proof garment, top quality shirts, speedy UK and worldwide delivery, and a friendly and efficient service. Together with our unconditional guarantee, this adds up to an unbeatable service.

(C) We hope that Tees Total will have the pleasure of printing for you in the future and look forward to hearing from you.

Yours sincerely,

Rachel Sturdy

Rachel Sturdy
TEES TOTAL

Enc.

Dictation

1 🔘 Listen to a reply to an enquiry about look-alikes of famous people.

a Who is the enquiry about?

b What do these expressions refer to?

– *we are pleased to enclose*
– *as early as possible*

2 You are a secretary. Listen and write down the letter.

Writing

You work at Jarvis International Gatwick, a hotel with conference facilities. You receive an enquiry from Alan Williams at Macrotech Computing. He needs a conference room on 14 October for ten people. He needs it for a full day. Write a reply to him at:

Unit 7, Westway Industrial Estate,
Warwick, CV4 7EF

Try to promote your service as in the letter opposite. Include the information below that you think is appropriate. The rooms below are available on 14 October at a cost of £48 per person.

conference rooms

Conferences featuring

Park View & Park Mews

Two stunning boardrooms for that Executive Board meeting, a small brainstorming session, or a private select dinner. Park View will cater for up to 12 people, whilst Park Mews can comfortably accommodate up to 10 persons.

Nearest Station
Three Bridges *2 miles*
Gatwick *4 miles*

Nearest Airport
Gatwick *4 miles*

Restaurant
There's a great choice of fine cuisine in

ARCHIPELAGO'S RESTAURANT

	Park View	Park Mews
Length Metres	6.3	7.5
Width Metres	3.4	3.4
Area SQ Metres	21.5	25.5
Max Height Metres	2.37	2.22
Soundproofed	✓	✓
No of 13 amp sockets	6	6
Telephone points	✓	✓

Park View	Park Mews
3.4m x 6.3m	3.4m x 7.5m

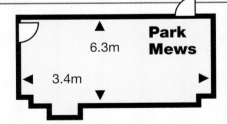

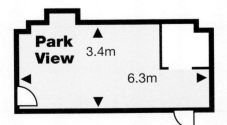

5C Telephone enquiries

Reading

Teresa and Marek are looking at a leaflet about gift packaging. They hope to get a special discount for a big order for the partners.

Teresa and Marek both decide to phone 'Just for You' to ask about special discounts. The person they want to speak to isn't there.

1 Look at the messages they leave. Which is the better message? Why?

TELEPHONE MESSAGE

To: Liz Parker
From: Marek Staniuk
Date: 10 December

Message: would like 40% discount on gift bags. Phone back on 0121-754-0574.

TELEPHONE MESSAGE

To: Liz Parker
From: Teresa Volpe
Date: 10 December

Message: would like to discuss a bulk order. Please phone back on 0181-313-1333.

JUST FOR YOU *offers an exclusive gift wrapping range which enables shops to offer stylish, co-ordinated wrapping. Gift bags and boxes are available in many designs.*

JUST FOR YOU *welcomes enquiries from distributors and agents.*

2 In a reply to a telephone enquiry, in what order do you:

a close the conversation?
b get through to the right person?
c give your reply?
d explain you are replying to an enquiry?
e say who you are and/or what company you work for?
f talk freely?

Listening

Liz Parker replies to her messages.

1 🔊 Listen to her conversation with Marek. Does Marek get what he wants?

2 Listen again.
  a How much discount does Marek ask for?
  b How much discount does Liz offer?
  c What does Marek say he will do?

3 🔊 Now listen to Liz Parker talking to Teresa. Is Teresa more successful than Marek?

4 Listen again, and fill in the missing words from the box opposite.

Pronunciation

In English it is usual to stress one or two important words in every sentence.

1 🔊 Listen and notice how the underlined words are stressed:

I've just opened a <u>gift</u> shop in <u>London</u>.
I'm looking for some <u>special</u> gift bags.

Now read these sentences and underline all the words you think should be stressed.

  a I thought your gift bags looked lovely.
  b The problem is the quantity and the discount.
  c Three of us want to order together.
  d But the thing is we already have an offer of a better price.
  e I was hoping for a thirty-five per cent discount.
  f We'd like them delivered before next Tuesday.

2 🔊 Listen to the words Teresa stresses. Then repeat the sentences.

Role-play

Student A
You are a buyer. See File 9 on page 87.

Student B
You are a supplier. See File 30 on page 93.

USEFUL LANGUAGE
The problem is … What we need is …
The thing is … But only if …
What we'd like is … I'm afraid …

to	from	speaking	afraid	to
in	at	returning	about	for

LIZ   Could I speak ¹____ Teresa Volpe, please?

TERESA ²____.

LIZ   This is Liz Parker. I'm calling from 'Just for You'. I'm ³____ your call.

TERESA Oh good. I've just opened a gift shop ⁴____ London. I saw your stand ⁵____ the Birmingham trade fair and I thought your gift bags looked lovely. I'm looking for some special gift bags. The problem is the quantity and the discount.

LIZ   I'm ⁶____ our maximum discount is usually twenty per cent ⁷____ a single order of a thousand packets.

TERESA Well, the quantity is fine, because three of us want to order together. But the thing is we already have the offer of a better price ⁸____ another company, which my partners are prepared to accept.

LIZ   Oh.

TERESA Well, I was hoping for a thirty-five per cent discount.

LIZ   Oh. Um … how ⁹____ twenty-five per cent?

TERESA Yes, okay, but only if you can deliver them ¹⁰____ three different addresses.

LIZ   Well, okay, as you're just starting.

TERESA Great. We'd like them delivered before next Tuesday, if that's …

Listening

Look at the problem and four possible solutions.

THE PROBLEM
How to make one gift shop stand out
to make it more attractive than the
competitors'. This is especially important
at Christmas when shops in the same
town often sell similar products.

POSSIBLE SOLUTIONS
A have beautiful window displays
B have really low prices
C offer free gifts to customers
D offer a good wrapping service

1 Listen to Silvia and Peter. Which of the ideas above do they mention?

2 Listen again and complete these sentences:
a _____ do something together?
b _____ decide on a free gift.
c _____ order a T-shirt.
d _____ we design our own?
e _____ we ask the others what they think?

3 Use the expressions above to discuss what to put on a free T-shirt for Perfect Partners' customers.

EXAMPLE
We could have a picture of a famous person.
What colours shall we use?

4 Write a slogan to put on the T-shirt.

▶ modals page 116

Reading

Teresa and Marek think a give-away T-shirt is a good idea too. Teresa shows the others the sales literature she received from Tees Total.

1 Read about the special offer and complete the flow chart opposite with words from the text.

TEES TOTAL
GARMENT ORDER FORM

HOW TO PLACE AN ORDER

1. We do not require payment with the order. Send us a £50.00 deposit (cheques payable to Tees Total) together with your artwork instructions and shirt order form (see over). Your deposit will be deducted when you are invoiced for your final order. Please note: we do not require a deposit for re-orders.

2. Upon receipt of this fully completed form we will send you an acknowledgement letter to let you know it has been safely received.

3. For new orders we will then send you a free sample printed with your design for your approval. For orders of less than 20 garments, if you require a sample, we charge £10.00 + VAT for this service.

4. When we have received full approval of your sample (together with your final order), we will send you an itemized costing and confirmation. Please note at this stage your order quantities can still be altered if required.

5. When we receive your final payment, we will print and dispatch your order. (Cheques / postal orders payable to Tees Total.)

Decide on an idea for a motif

Send three things:

a

b

c

After 3 / 4 days receive:

d

Design process: 2 weeks

Receive:

e

Decide on quantity: 1 week

Send two things:

f

g

Wait 4 days.

Receive:

h

Send:

i

Processing: postal order 4 days or cheque 10 days

Printing: 5 days

Dispatch: 2 days

Receive T-shirts

2 According to the flow chart, how long will it take to:
- **a** prepare the sample garment?
- **b** send the invoice?
- **c** print and dispatch the T-shirts?

3 How long will the whole process take?

4 When do the partners have to start if:
- **a** they want the T-shirts by mid-November?
- **b** they allow an extra three weeks for delays?

Grammar
when + present simple

1 Look at these sentences about the offer:

When Tees Total receive the deposit and motif, they will design the T-shirt.

Will they print all the T-shirts when they receive the motif?

– **Which event happens first?**
– **What is the word that links the two parts of the sentence?**
– **Which tense is used in each part of the sentence?**

2 Underline the correct form of the verbs in brackets.

EXAMPLE
Tees Total (send / will send) a final invoice when you (will submit / submit) your final order.

- **a** When you (pay / will pay) the final invoice, Tees Total (will print / print) all the T-shirts.
- **b** How long (it take / will it take) Tees Total to print the sample after they (will receive / receive) the motif?
- **c** How long (it take / will it take) before you (will receive / receive) all the T-shirts?
- **d** I (am / will be) there before you (will arrive / arrive).

▸ **future time clauses** page 115
▸ **conjunctions** page 113

6B Orders

Writing

1 Find the words and expressions on the form that mean:

- **a** liquid used in printing and writing
- **b** say
- **c** complete (vb)
- **d** exchange of letters
- **e** an image or a picture
- **f** do not write here
- **g** money left as security
- **h** magazine or newspaper
- **i** second or further order
- **j** accept

2 Now you fill in the form. Invent appropriate details.

3 Now design an order form yourself. The form is to go at the back of a mail order clothing catalogue and should include details of the order:

- – garment size and colour
- – credit card number
- – name and address, etc.

Reading

Buying and selling is more complicated in international trade. *Documentary credit* is one method of payment which protects both the supplier and the buyer.

Read the text, then complete the flow chart with the numbers relating to the stages in the text.

1 The importer agrees to pay for goods by documentary credit, and tells his bank that he will do so by completing an application form.

2 The importer's bank selects a bank in the exporter's country and sends them notification that the credit has been opened.

3 The exporter's bank sends notification to the exporter that credit has been opened.

4 The exporter (a) ships the goods before the credit expires and (b) sends the shipping documents (i.e. the Bill of Lading*, the insurance certificate, and invoice) to the exporter's bank.

For office use only

Date received _____ Artwork No. _____ Order No. _____

Date sample sent _____ Shirt type _____

The Tees Total Offer Printed Garment Order Form

Please use ink to fill in the form.

Name: Mr / Mrs / Miss / Ms

Date   Telephone No.

Name of club / business etc.

Full name and address for correspondence / delivery

Is this a re-order?   Yes   No

Delivery date final order is required?

Please tick the relevant boxes
(this section is not applicable for re-orders).

I enclose my deposit of £50

Official purchase order

Before you print my order I would like to approve:

1 A photocopy of my finished design

2 A sample garment printed with my own design

Sample garment details (if required):

T-shirt / sweatshirt / other   Size

Colour

Please state in which publication you saw our advertisement:

Use space provided overleaf for your artwork instructions.

Thank you for your order.

When complete, send this form to:
Tees Total, 153 High Street, Wooton Bassett, Nr. Swindon, Wilts SN4 7AB.

5 After checking the documents, the exporter's bank pays the exporter.

6 The exporter's bank then sends the documents to the importer's bank.

7 After checking the documents, the importer's bank (a) pays the exporter's bank, and (b) sends the documents to the importer.

8 When the importer receives his copy of the documents, he can collect the goods that have now arrived.

* a Bill of Lading is a document used for goods that are shipped

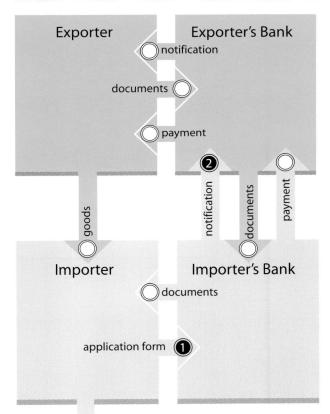

Grammar
passives

1 Look at these sentences:

The importer's bank checks the documents.
The documents are checked.

– Which sentence focuses only on the action?
– Which tells us who is responsible for the action?

We use the passive when we do not know, or it is not important, who does / did something.

2 Rewrite these sentences using the passive.

EXAMPLE
The importer's bank selects a bank in the exporter's country.

A bank in the exporter's country is selected (by the importer's bank).

a The exporter's bank notifies the exporter. *The exporter …*
b The exporter ships the goods. *The goods …*
c The exporter's bank sends the documents to the importer's bank. *The documents …*
d The importer collects the goods when he / she receives the documents. *The goods …*

▶ **passives** page 117

Dictation

Marek is importing some watches from Switzerland.

1 Listen to the letter he writes about the method of payment. Match the numbers in Column **A** to the items in Column **B**.

A		B	
1	28	a	the order number
2	200	b	a date in March
3	26–45	c	the value of the irrevocable
4	6698		letter of credit
5	20	d	a date in January
6	6000	e	the number of watches ordered
		f	the catalogue numbers

2 Listen again and write down the letter.

6C Be prepared

TELEPHONE CALL – PREPARATION

Company	TEES TOTAL
Number	01793 849888
Person	MR WILSON
Extension number	336

Expressions I might need to get through

Can you put me through to the sales department, please?

Could I speak to mr ... please?

I think he's on extension number ...

Things I need to ask

1. Could we use our own design?

2. When will we get the proof garment?

3. Will Tees Total accept a faxed instruction as proof of payment?

Expressions I may need to explain and check things

my colleague ... wrote to you recently and we received your sales material.

your letter was dated ...

I need some further information about ...

We understand ... Is that right?

We are a little anxious about the delivery times.

If we order by ... will we receive the goods by ... ?

It's really important for us.

At the latest.

By return of post.

Can you confirm ...

Do we have to ... ?

Thank you, mr ... You have been most helpful.

Listening

Efficient people prepare themselves before making a phone call. Silvia is going to phone Tees Total to check some points. Look at the points she wants to check and at the useful expressions.

1 ▭ Listen and tick (✓) the expressions she uses.

2 Listen again. Number the expressions she uses in the order she uses them.

3 Listen again. Note down the answers to her three questions.

Grammar
requests

1 Look at these questions:

Could you confirm that, please?
Can we design our own T-shirts?

– Which one asks for permission? Which asks someone to do something?

– Which words tell us?

2 Decide which of these questions ask for permission:

a Can you put me through to the sales department, please?

b Could we send £50 now and the rest next week?

c Can I let you know tomorrow?

d Could you tell me the way to the accounts department, please?

e Can you give me some information about accommodation, please?

f Can I open the window, please?

3 Which of the requests above are more formal than the others? Why?

4 Make the other requests more formal.

▶ **modals** page 116

Pronunciation

Some words sound different if they are not stressed.

1 📼 Listen to these sentences. How is *can* pronounced?

How can I help you?
We can send the invoice immediately.

2 Now read this dialogue with a partner. Is *can* pronounced /kən/ or /kæn/?

A Can you confirm that we will receive the goods by Friday?

B Yes, I can. The goods will be with you on Thursday.

A And can we send them back if we don't like them?

B You certainly can. But you have to send them back the same day.

3 📼 Listen and check your answers.

Role-play

Work in pairs. Each write a telephone call preparation sheet for a different situation. Use the preparation sheet on the opposite page.

Student A
See File 10 on page 87 for your information.

Student B
See File 31 on page 93 for your information.

USEFUL LANGUAGE
I've already placed an order for …
I'm interested in placing …
Can you tell me …?
I'm interested in the trade fair in …
I would like to know if …
I'm really sorry about this. I suggest you call …
I appreciate how you feel.
Is there a discount for bigger orders?
If I order … will you …?
Can you give me any information about accommodation?

Listening

After one of their regular meetings, Teresa invites Marek and Silvia to dinner in her flat in London. Peter helps Teresa with the cooking.

1 Who do you think says the things below: the guests (Silvia and Marek) or the hosts (Peter and Teresa)? Write *H* (hosts) or *G* (guests).

  a What a lovely room! ___G___
  b Let me take your coat. ___H___
  c I hope you like Italian food. _____
  d Can I use your bathroom? _____
  e Would you like some more pasta? _____
  f This is for you. I hope you like it. _____
  g I've brought you some chocolates. _____
  h That was delicious. _____
  i You have some wonderful things. _____

2 ▭ There is a beautiful Turkish rug on the wall in the dining room. Listen. Who bought it?

3 Listen again.

  a How much did the man originally want for the wall hanging?

  b How much did he accept in the end?
  c How does Peter feel about bargaining?
  d And Teresa?

4 Do you have a story to tell about bargaining?

USEFUL LANGUAGE
The asking price was …
It cost £10.
The man wanted £15 for it.
That was too much. I offered …
In the end he brought the price down.
In the end I got it for less.
I paid him £8 for it.

▶ **money** page 116

5 ▭ In some cultures it is normal to bargain. Listen to two stories about bargaining in different countries. Which has a happier ending?

6 Listen again and note down:

  a the original asking prices.
  b the prices the customers paid in the end.

Reading

1 What gifts do guests take to their hosts in your country?

2 Read the following story and complete it with these verbs in the simple past:

want	buy	ring	go
look	be	can	give
ask	thank	explain	start

▶ **irregular verbs** page 122

I was in Italy on business in late October and I was invited to dinner by an Italian business colleague. I ¹_____ to take her a present so I ²_____ to the market to buy some flowers. As I said, it was late October and so the chrysanthemums ³_____ especially beautiful. I ⁴_____ some magnificent yellow ones. Then I went to my colleague's house and ⁵_____ the bell. When she opened the door, I ⁶_____ her the flowers, and I smiled. But I ⁷_____ tell that something was wrong because her face ⁸_____ so strange. She ⁹_____ me politely but I could see she wasn't pleased.

Later I ¹⁰_____ my friend about it. 'What flowers did you buy?' he asked. 'Chrysanthemums,' I replied, and he ¹¹_____ laughing. 'What's the joke?' I asked, and he ¹²_____ that in Italy November 2nd is the Day of the Dead and everyone takes chrysanthemums to the cemetery to decorate the family tomb. No one has them in the house.

3 Why were the chrysanthemums not an appropriate present?

4 If you want to do business in a foreign country:
  a which of the topics below do you think you should know a lot about?
  b which of the topics are 'safe' to discuss with someone from a different culture?

- religion
- the family
- style of dress
- holidays
- history
- punctuality
- food and drink
- education system
- entertainment
- spending habits
- politics
- geography
- special customs

5 In pairs, tell each other a story of a misunderstanding between two different cultures. Each of you has a part of the story.

Student A
Look at the instructions in File 11 on page 88.

Student B
Look at the instructions in File 32 on page 94.

Reading

1 Read this article by Peter Cochrane of British Telecom about e-mail, then say what the following expressions refer to:

a less than 5 a week
b 660 people
c 98%
d in 12 hours
e 3 years
f within 3½ hours
g 12 a day

EXAMPLE
'Less than 5 a week' refers to the number of letters he now writes each week.

2 Ask about any other expressions you don't understand.

Switching to Electronic Communications

Peter Cochrane
is Head of Advanced Applications and Technologies at BT, and a dedicated e-mailer. He describes the impact of switching to electronic communications.

Six hundred and sixty people work in my department. Three years ago I started an experiment. I told the 660 people that I would respond to any electronic message in no more than 12 hours, and that I would destroy all internal paper correspondence.

Statistically, the change has been dramatic. On average, I now respond to all communications within about 3½ hours. I respond to nearly all of my external communications electronically and complete 98% of them within 12 hours. The number of letters I write has gone from an average of 12 a day to less than 5 a week. I send far more e-mails than I did letters, but I spend less time doing it because it can be less formal, more concise, and more direct.

3 Look at the e-mail message below.

a When was it sent?
b What is it about?
c Would you write this style of e-mail to a friend?

To	2/1/00 4:35pm

clarkel, peplerm,alvarengav

Subject

COMMITTEE MEETING

I'm afraid Mr Griffin will not be in Britain on 12th January and so the meeting is rescheduled to the 25th at 10.00. Please check your availability and confirm. Thank you.
Margaret

4 Look at these e-mail messages between the Perfect Partners.

a Put in the missing articles in the first e-mail: *a* or *th*
b Which of the partners (Silvia, Marek, Teresa, Peter) do the letters A, B, C, D refer to?

▶ **articles** page 112

①

Subject

Want some fun?

Message

Hi, (A) _____
Guess what! We entered ¹_____ competition in ²_____ magazine and we won! ³_____ prize is two places on ⁴ _l_ business course. It looks really good. It runs from October 15–17 and it will be held near Gatwick Airport. The hotel has ⁵_____ swimming pool. Teresa and I want to share ⁶_____ prize between ⁷_____ four of us. It costs £500 ⁸_____ head so we would each have to pay £250. What do you think? It would be nice to have our next meeting somewhere good. Will you come? I'll fax you ⁹_____ details if you're interested.

With best wishes – and hoping to see you again very soon.

(B) _____

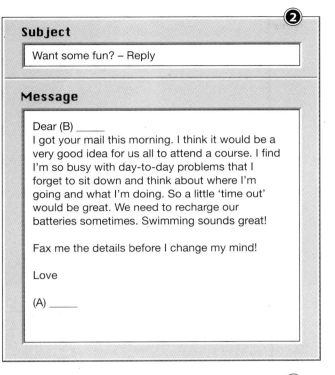

② Subject

Want some fun? – Reply

Message

Dear (B) _____
I got your mail this morning. I think it would be a very good idea for us all to attend a course. I find I'm so busy with day-to-day problems that I forget to sit down and think about where I'm going and what I'm doing. So a little 'time out' would be great. We need to recharge our batteries sometimes. Swimming sounds great!

Fax me the details before I change my mind!

Love

(A) _____

④ Subject

Course in England

Message

Hi there, (D) _____
This is your perfect partner from London! Listen, we've won some places on a business course. We were really surprised. We entered a competition in a retailers' magazine and we won first prize – two places on this course. We'd like to share our prize with our perfect partners. So we suggest that we all go on the course and pay half each – partners should share! I faxed you the details but then I forgot to mail you to explain what it's all about. Typical! Sometimes Peter is more efficient than I am.

Bye, (C) _____

③ Subject

What's going on?

Message

Hey, (C) _____ , I got a really strange fax from you this morning. A business course near Gatwick Airport?! It looks really good, but isn't it a bit expensive? You only sent the brochure, so I don't understand what you have in mind. Do you think I should go on this course? Are you going on it? Get back to me soon because the deadline for applications is tomorrow.

(D) _____

⑤ Subject

Now I understand!!

Message

(C) _____
Great idea! And I'd love to see you again. And if we're in the same hotel, we can all spend the evenings together as well. What about Silvia? Does she agree with the idea? I think Silvia would like to see Peter again! What do you think?

C-Ya,

(D) _____

Dictation

Your boss comes into your office and asks you to e-mail a client to say that their consignment has been dispatched.

1 🔲 Listen. When was it dispatched?

2 Listen and write the e-mail message.

Writing

1 You are Steven Mason (see Dictation). Reply to Brad Nelson by e-mail.

2 You see an ad on the Internet for a friendship club for learning English. E-mail to ask for further details.

7C Mobile phones

Listening

1 When you call someone on a mobile phone, you don't know where that person is or what they are doing, so you have to check.

Hello. Am I disturbing you?
No, no, I'm just having some tea in the kitchen.

Invent similar conversations. Go round the class. Each student should invent a different answer.

2 ▭ Listen to a conversation between Peter and his friend Jack. Decide if the following are true or false, and write *T* or *F* after each sentence.

a Jack is in the office. _____
b Jack has two mobile phones. _____
c Both his mobile phones are for personal use. _____
d Peter wanted to know someone's address. _____
e Jack doesn't have the information with him. _____
f There are some horses in a field outside the window. _____
g There is also a red tractor. _____
h Peter and Jack are going to meet in the restaurant. _____

3 Put the verbs in the right tense.

EXAMPLE
Who (call)?
Who's calling?

a (I disturb) you?
b (you remember) that man at the party?
c (you have) his number?
d (you go) somewhere nice?
e Excuse me – that's my other mobile (ring).
f (I go) on some course this weekend to improve my business skills.

4 Below are two scrambled mobile phone conversations. One is between a courier and his depot; the other is between two business people. Unscramble them.

a Hi, Bill. We were worried. Aren't you coming to the meeting?
b Susan, this is Mick. I can't find the right office for that small parcel, and it's raining.

c Great, thanks.
d Fine. See you later then. Bye.
e I'm outside the main entrance of the main building.
f Okay. We'll start without you then.
g Poor Mick. Where are you now?
h Yes, I am. I'm just ringing to say I'll be a few minutes late.
i Right. Go round to the back of that building. There are two doors … (*the line crackles*)
j Hello, is that Jeff? This is Bill.
k That's better. Right, there are two doors. You want the second one. Then call them on the intercom.
l I can't hear you properly. The line's … breaking up … (*the line breaks*). Hello?

5 ▭ Listen and check your answers.

Pronunciation

Some words sound different when they are next to other words.

1 ▭ Listen to the following phrases from the telephone call between Peter and Jack. What do you notice about the underlined sounds?

a Is it a good time to call?
b … wasn't doing …
c I wanted to ask you …
d The one who sells special cards.
e … business skills.
f And a red tractor.

2 🔊 Where do sounds 'disappear' in the following?

a Thank goodness!

b A bunch of flowers!

c She's Susan.

d A big car.

e What do you do?

f A top business person.

Grammar
must and *might*

1 Look at these sentences:

We might be on the same train.
We must be on the same train.

– **Which of them means the same as:**
Perhaps we are on the same train?

– **Which means the same as:**
I'm sure we are on the same train?

2 Underline the correct word.

EXAMPLE
He has a sports car, five houses, and a private jet.
He must / might be rich.

a His boss asked him to go to her office immediately.
She (must / might) want to speak to him about something urgent.

b The sky is cloudy.
It looks as if it (must / might) rain.

c That retail chain is opening a new outlet.
They (must / might) need new staff.

d I heard that three companies are closing in that town.
Business (must / might) be bad.

e They are going to merge the two companies.
They (must / might) make some staff redundant.

▸ modals page 116

Speaking

Teresa is on the train with Peter and Jack. A friend, Isabel, is looking after the shop while they are away. Teresa calls her.

Look at this summary of their conversation. What do you think they actually say?

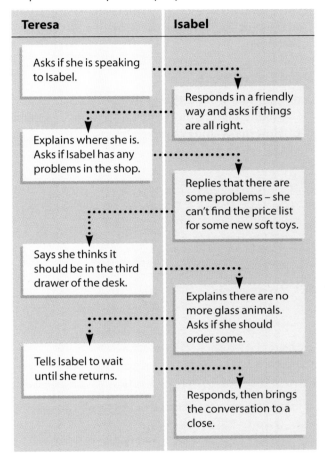

Teresa	Isabel
Asks if she is speaking to Isabel.	
	Responds in a friendly way and asks if things are all right.
Explains where she is. Asks if Isabel has any problems in the shop.	
	Replies that there are some problems – she can't find the price list for some new soft toys.
Says she thinks it should be in the third drawer of the desk.	
	Explains there are no more glass animals. Asks if she should order some.
Tells Isabel to wait until she returns.	
	Responds, then brings the conversation to a close.

Role-play

In pairs, role-play mobile phone conversations.

Student A
Look at the instructions in File 12 on page 88.

Student B
Look at the instructions in File 33 on page 94.

USEFUL LANGUAGE
Am I disturbing you?
No, no, I'm just …
In fact, I'm rather busy.
Well, actually …
Could I call you back …

8A A business course

Speaking

The first session of the course is about Time Management. Before it starts, the participants are asked to write down the following:

— a list of everything they did on the Wednesday before the course
— three sentences describing what is most important to them in their work in the form of a Mission Statement.

1 Read what Peter wrote.

a How many of the things that he did last Wednesday conflict with his Mission Statement?

b How many things support it?

Last Wednesday I:

- had the morning off and cleaned my flat.

- rushed out at 1.00 p.m. to buy a suit to wear on the course.

- went to the shop (1.45 p.m.) and spent half an hour arguing with Teresa about her window display.

- checked Teresa's correspondence at 2.45 p.m. and had to change the dates on three orders (!!), then faxed them again.

- chatted to an Australian friend, who came in at 3.30 p.m., for 30 minutes, then went for a coffee (4.00-5.00 p.m.).

- talked to an African student who came in with some nice things to sell.

- closed the shop at 5.30 p.m.

Mission Statement

- to work in a pleasant, relaxed and peaceful environment.

- to make shopping a pleasant experience for my customers.

- to find really unusual gifts to sell in the shop.

2 Complete these questions with the words below:

What was	Did
How long did	Did
How many	How much
Were	What did

a _____ the first thing you did on Wednesday?
b _____ it take?
c _____ you do next?
d _____ it take long?
e _____ hours did you work?
f _____ time did you spend on yourself?
g _____ you pleased with your day's work?
h _____ you do anything that was in conflict with your Mission Statement?

▶ **questions** page 120
▶ **past simple** page 118

3 What do you think Peter's answers to the above questions are?

Role-play

In pairs, role-play conversations about Silvia and Marek's Mission Statements and about what they did on the Wednesday before the course.

Student A
You are Silvia. Look at the instructions in File 13 on page 88.

Student B
You are Marek. Look at the instructions in File 34 on page 94.

Reading

Time management in business is very important. It means thinking hard about who should do what and when.

1 Below is a list of tasks to do in one day in a recording studio. You are the manager.

a Which tasks could your assistant do? Which ones should you do personally?

b Complete the diary below.

1 Meet the manager of a promising new group (10.00–11.00 a.m.).

2 Stick new labels on all your cassettes.

3 Call one of your suppliers (you have cash flow problems).

4 Talk to one of the sound technicians – some poor work recently.

5 Address envelopes and post invitations to a publicity function.

6 Prepare for an important meeting with the bank next week.

7 Meeting at (3.15–4.00 p.m.) to plan recording schedule.

8 Lunch (1.30–2.00 p.m.) with one of your partners – he's a bit depressed.

▶ modals page 116

2 After a long day talking about themselves, Silvia and Teresa are having a swim and talking about Peter. Listen.

a Who really likes Peter?

b Do Peter and Teresa have the same friends?

3 ▭ Listen to Marek and Jack talking about the others.

a Who does Marek really like?

b What happened between Jack and Teresa?

Grammar
questions with *who*

1 Look at these two questions:

Who really likes Peter?
Who does Marek really like?

Which one asks about the *subject*? … the *object*?

2 The underlined word is the answer. Write the question.

EXAMPLE
Managers listen to <u>their employees</u>.
Who do managers listen to?

a <u>The new secretary</u> reports directly to the Sales Manager.

b Peter met <u>Marek</u> at the trade fair.

c <u>The Managing Director</u> gave everyone a pay rise.

d Teresa is waiting for <u>Peter</u>.

e <u>The company</u> sends free gifts to its customers.

f The Sales Manager gave a presentation to <u>a new client</u>.

▶ questions page 120

8B Presentation

Speaking

One session on the business course was about letterheads and logos.

1 Look at the fonts and choose adjectives from this list to describe them:

> elegant   modern   fun
> old-fashioned   professional

a

b

c

d

e

2 Say which ones would be suitable for the letterhead of:

  a a classy clothes shop
  b a farm offering bed and breakfast
  c a recording studio
  d a clothes shop for young people
  e a government agency

3 This leaflet is for a company which sells printed mousemats but it doesn't look very professional.

  a Find mistakes in the following:

    – spelling (2)
    – punctuation (2)
    – capital letters (2)

  EXAMPLE
  They must correct the spelling of 'road'.

  b Suggest improvements in the presentation:

    – picture
    – letterhead
    – layout

  EXAMPLE
  They should put 'Special Offer' first.

Mouse Mat Mad
12 Welburn Raoad
Fax

Are you looking for new ways to promote your company. Well, you don't need to look any further – we have the solution!!

Mouse mats can be printed with your compani name and address. Now your clients won't have to waste their time looking for your number in a phone book – they will always have it at their fingertips?

first 10 free if you order more than 50 but you must place your order before the end of april.

All you have to do is pick up the fone and dial : 01870–556620

or e-mail us at: mousematmad@compaccess.co.uk

All you need to send us is a description of the information and / or images you want us to print.

!!!!!Special Offer!!!!!

Grammar
must and should

1 Look at these sentences:

I think they should put 'Special Offer' first.
They must correct the spelling of 'road'.

Which one is stronger, *should* or *must*?

2 Tell someone what to do about these problems:

EXAMPLE
There is a mistake on this invoice. (correct)
You must correct it.

a He doesn't like his job.
(look for a new one)
b We have no new customers.
(attract new ones)
c The sales team wants to go to China.
(apply for visas)
d They want to do some sightseeing.
(buy a guide book)
e Silvia has a lot of work.
(get an assistant)
f Teresa has made a lot of typing errors.
(correct them)

▶ modals page 116

Writing

Incorrect use of capital letters in written English is another cause of bad presentation in commercial correspondence.

1 Why are capital letters used in these sentences?

a I studied Spanish and Italian at London University.
b Liz Parker is Sales Manager at 'Just for You' in London.
c I saw your ad for a new PA in The Evening Standard.
d My address is 26 West Street, London NW7, England.
e And I was born on Friday, 9 June.

2 Rewrite these sentences using capital letters.

a our new address in edinburgh is 31 east road.
b the next meeting will be on Thursday, august 31st at 10 o'clock in the morning.
c we read the times every day and the economist every week.
d marek is managing director of the anglo-polish import-export company.
e he's german but he now lives in the usa.

3 You work for a recording studio. Write a sales letter including the information below:

– **Letterhead:**
Hip Hop Recording, 97 Kings Road, London
Tel: 0171–988899, Fax: 0171–998899

– **Special Offer:**
12.5% price reduction, established clients

– **Terms and conditions:**
book end of month, no deposit

– **Opening times and contacts:**
8.30–5.30, Mike or Sasha

– **Other information:**
new mixing equipment

Dictation

1 Read the letter below.

Dear Mr Smith,

As one of our most valued customers, we wanted you to be the first to know about our new range and so we are sending you our updated catalogue. Take a close look at page 23. We are sure that it will interest you. We also have some interesting new products in our outdoor wear line.

To show that we value your custom we will continue to offer you a 25% discount and hope to receive your orders soon.

2 🔲 Listen to your boss's instructions and note down the changes she wants.

3 Write the two new letters.

8C Good telephone manners

Listening

In business, it is important to give a good impression on the telephone.

1 Complete these suggestions with *Do* or *Don't*.

  a _____ sound positive!
  b _____ keep a caller waiting!
  c _____ give your name or the name of the company in a friendly voice!
  d _____ speak clearly!
  e _____ sound bored!
  f _____ give the impression you know very little about your company!
  g _____ apologize immediately if an apology is needed!
  h _____ get irritated!
  i _____ give the caller the name of the person you are going to put them through to!
  j _____ sound helpful!
  k _____ take responsibility: either solve the caller's problem or promise to take some appropriate action!
  l _____ break promises!

2 ▭ Listen to this receptionist. Which of these rules does she break?

3 Listen again. When your teacher stops the cassette, say what is wrong and why.

4 Expressions with *get* are often used in the place of other verbs. For example, *don't get irritated* means *don't become irritated*.

Rewrite the following sentences with one of these words:

find	buy	coming
contact	ask	ring

  a I'll *get back to* you as soon as I can.
  b Just a moment, he's out of the office. I'll *get* him for you.
  c What time is Mr X *getting* back? He'll be back at three.
  d I'll *get* him to call you back.
  e I can't *get through to* the supplier – their line's always engaged.
  f Can you *get* me a sandwich, please?

Grammar
common errors

There are a number of common mistakes that students make when speaking on the phone. You will sound professional if you avoid them.

1 Try correcting the following:

  a Hello. I am John Smith speaking.
  b I call from Spain.
  c I would to speak to John.
  d You send a brochure to me, please?
  e I send you a brochure immediately.
  f I look forward to see you next week.
  g Can I leave message, please?
  h Could I speak to Mrs Susan?

Pronunciation

Practise your best telephone manner.

🔲 Listen and repeat the following. Smile as you do so.

a I'll get him to call you back.
b I'll get back to you as soon as I can.
c Thank you for calling Perfect Partners.
d Hold the line, please. I'm putting you through.
e How can I help you?
f Have a nice day.

Speaking

1 Choose the correct alternative so that this is a polite conversation.

RECEPTIONIST	Good morning, Stone and Sons. / Yes, what do you want?
CALLER	Oh hello. I'd like to speak to James Stone.
RECEPTIONIST	He's not here. / I'm afraid he's not here today.
CALLER	Oh dear.
RECEPTIONIST	Call back tomorrow. / Shall I ask him to call you tomorrow?
CALLER	Yes, fine.
RECEPTIONIST	Can I take your name and number, please? / Who is it?

2 Match the mistakes with these comments:

1 The present simple is not used for actions which are happening now. The present continuous is needed here.
2 *Would* is not followed by *to*. *Would like* can be followed by *to* if the meaning is similar to *want*.
3 *Look forward to* should be followed by *-ing*.
4 This is a promise so *I'll* should be used, not the present simple.
5 Only surnames are used after titles like *Mr / Mrs / Ms / Dr*, not first names.
6 This form isn't used. On the telephone, say *This is … speaking.*
7 This is a request, so you should use *Can you …?* or the more polite *Could you …?*
8 The article *a* is missing.

2 Role-play 'good' and 'bad' telephone calls.

Student A
You are the customer.
See File 14 on page 88.

Student B
You are a shop assistant.
See File 35 on page 94.

3 Change roles.

Student A
You are a receptionist.
See File 15 on page 89.

Student B
You are the customer.
See File 36 on page 95.

9A Transporting goods

Reading

Silvia orders 150 waistcoats from a company in Boston, USA. She wants them for sale at Christmas which is in three months' time. Study this information about transport for goods.

1 Which method would be the best for this order? Why?

2 If Silvia chose this method, would the goods be delivered to her shop?

▼ By sea	▼ By air	▼ By rail	▼ By road
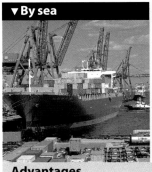			
Advantages			
– good for very long distances – inexpensive – cost is calculated by volume	– very fast	– fast	– door to door – fairly fast over land – not expensive
Disadvantages			
– slow – goods must be taken to and from port	– expensive – goods must be taken to and from airport	– fairly expensive – goods must be taken to and from station	– accidents and theft more common – delays at frontiers outside EU
Main transport document			
Bill of Lading (B/L or blading)	Air Waybill (AWB)	consignment note and Single Administrative Document (SAD) for customs	consignment note and Single Administrative Document (SAD) for customs
Typical goods carried			
most things	ideal for perishable items, such as food, and goods of high value	ideal for large quantities of heavy goods	most things except very large quantities and oversize goods

Listening

Silvia decides to have the waistcoats sent by sea.

1 Look at the *Bill of Lading*. What details are missing?

2 ▭ The supplier phones the shipping agent. Listen and complete the bill.

3 Listen again and write down all the questions.

4 In pairs, ask and answer the same questions.

5 Which of the phrases below would you expect to see on containers with these products?

  a acid
  b stereo equipment
  c clothes
  d plastic bottles of fruit juice
  e glass vases
  f insecticide

Shipper	**BILL OF LADING**	
Western Merchant Lines	B/L No.	2003 3970
	Reference No.	NE 234 70

Consignor
Waistcoats

Consignee (or state 'order' to notify address)
Order

Notify address
Silvia Adario, Gran Via, 2022, 08042, Barcelona, Spain
Tel:

Vessel	Port of loading
The North Encounter	No. 4 Dock, Boston

Port of discharge	Place of delivery by on-carrier

Freight payable at	Number of original Bs/L

Gross weight	Measurement

Marks and numbers	Number and kind of packages; description of goods
Keep Dry	3 boxes clothing items

THIS SIDE UP

CORROSIVE

FRAGILE

POISON

KEEP DRY

HANDLE WITH CARE

9B Letters of complaint

Reading

Silvia's waistcoats are damaged in transit. She sends a formal letter of complaint about the damaged goods.

1 Match the words in column **A** with the definitions in column **B**.

A	B
a complain	not in a good enough condition to sell
b consignment	to guess / to judge
c compensation	say you are unhappy about goods or services
d shipment	an organization which arranges transportation
e unsaleable	quantity of goods to be transported by ship
f forwarding company	a load of goods ordered by a customer
g estimate	repayment for loss / damage suffered

2 Now complete Silvia's letter with the words above.

Dear Mr Hilton,

I am writing to ¹_____ about the ²_____ of waistcoats which I received yesterday, ten days late.

The cardboard boxes in which the waistcoats were packed were badly damaged. After a quick inspection, I ³_____ that most of the items are ⁴_____ and I am, therefore, returning the whole ⁵_____.

I suggest you contact the ⁶_____ and ask them for full ⁷_____. Fortunately, the sale was on a CIF basis. Please let me have a full replacement consignment as soon as possible.

Yours sincerely,

Silvia Adario

Silvia Adario

*CIF: cost, freight, and insurance

3 A typical letter of complaint is in three paragraphs:
- the first paragraph states the reason for writing
- the second paragraph explains the problem
- the third paragraph suggests a solution.

Below are nine paragraphs from three different letters. They are not in the right order.

a First, find the three opening paragraphs. What are the three causes for complaint?

b Now find the paragraphs to complete each letter and copy the three letters.

1 I have returned everything by post this morning. I would be most grateful if you could send us the new consignment by express delivery.

2 I am writing with reference to Order No. CV537 of 3 September, because it was incomplete on arrival this morning.

3 As soon as I opened the boxes, I realized you had sent us men's shirts and not women's.

4 I will keep the damaged items in our warehouse for a few days, in case you wish to send someone to inspect them.

5 I am faxing you to complain about a consignment of glass vases that I have just received, my order No. KL889.

6 The moment I opened the first chest, I noticed that many items were missing. These include two complete hi-fis and three sets of loud speakers.

7 Unfortunately, when I unpacked them, I found several items were broken.

8 We would like to inform you that you have sent us the wrong items.

9 If the whole consignment does not arrive before October 1st, the order will be cancelled and we will find another supplier.

Grammar
time conjunctions

1 Find examples of three of these time conjunctions in **3** opposite and underline them.

when
as soon as
the minute
the moment

– What is the tense of the verb that is used with them?

2 Join these sentences using the words in brackets and put the verb in the correct tense:

EXAMPLE
I (open) the sack. I (notice) a mouse. (when)
*When I **opened** the sack I **noticed** a mouse.*

a I (unpack) the boxes. I (find) several items were broken. (when)

b They (send) a fax. They (receive) the consignment. (as soon as)

c I (see) the damage. I (phone) the supplier. (as soon as)

d He (see) the money was missing. He (open) the safe. (the minute)

▶ conjunctions page 113

Dictation

Listen to this reply to a letter of complaint.

1 In what order do you think the phrases below are mentioned?

a In the meantime ____
b We do appreciate the problems ____
c June 9th ____
d Could you please return ____
e However, I am pleased to say ____

2 Listen and check your answers.

3 Listen again and write the letter down.

Writing

Use some of the expressions in the letters opposite, or similar ones, to write two letters of complaint.

1 Write a very polite letter about an incomplete delivery of shoes (you ordered 60 pairs but received 35 pairs). They are needed urgently. You are worried because the winter season has begun. You need to know when you can expect the other shoes.

2 Write a hostile letter (but not rude or personal) about a computer system. Some of the accessories were missing. You are angry because it was a present for someone and your customer has refused to take it or wait for a replacement. You want someone to take it away immediately, or else …!

9C Solving problems by phone

Listening

Silvia phones George Hilton the manager of the waistcoat company in Boston.

1 🔲 Listen. What do these numbers refer to?

EXAMPLE
Seventy-five is the number of waistcoats that Silvia asked for.

a 75 _____
b 50 _____
c 25 _____
d 20th _____
e 17th _____

2 Listen again. Underline the word Silvia stresses most in each of these sentences:

a But I need them now.
b Yes, but my goods were damaged.
c Can't you do something about it?
d Can't you help me?

3 Which of these promises does George Hilton make?

a I'll talk to my production manager.
b I'll send you a fax tomorrow.
c I'll get back to you later in the day.
d I'll send someone to the airport with them.
e I'll take them to the airport myself.
f I'll ask someone to bring them to your shop.
g I'll see what I can do.
h And I'll be in touch later.

▶ **future** page 114

Grammar
as many as / as much as

1 Look at these dialogues:

> A: *I ordered some glue.*
> B: *Has it arrived yet?*
> A: *Yes, but not as much as I ordered.*

> A: *I ordered some pens last week.*
> B: *Have they arrived yet?*
> A: *Yes, but not as many as I ordered.*

– Why is *much* used in the first dialogue and *many* in the second?

2 Complete these sentences with *much* or *many*.

a I can lend you some money, but I don't have as _____ as you need.
b Two hundred H4 pencils? I'm afraid we don't have as _____ as that in stock.

3 Use *as much as* or *as many as* to talk about problems with each of the products below.

EXAMPLE
Have the books arrived yet?
Not as many as you ordered.

books   paper   spray paint
glasses   ink   envelopes
photocopier toner

▶ **countable and uncountable nouns** page 113

Reading

Silvia and George handled their conversation professionally.

1 Read the following extracts from five similar conversations. Which two are unprofessional?

a I'm really sorry about this! I do apologize. But …

b I really appreciate how you feel about this. My advice is to call Mr Smith. He's in charge of shipping.

c I'm afraid we're having some problems with production. One of our suppliers is delivering late.

d Tell me exactly what the problem is and I'll see what I can do.

e Well, there's nothing I can do about it. It's not my fault. You'll have to speak to Mr Smith. It's his department.

2 Look at these reactions to the above extracts. Match them.

EXAMPLE

1 e

1 How rude! ____

2 That's *your* problem. What about mine? ____

3 It's nice when they appreciate my problems. Now for Mr Smith! ____

4 She sounds practical. Perhaps she'll help me solve this problem. ____

5 Yes? 'But' what? ____

Pronunciation

We stress the important words in a sentence and words which give new information.

1 Read this dialogue. Underline the words which are stressed in each line.

A I'm afraid we only have fifty available today.

B But I asked for seventy.

A I know but they could only send us fifty. The other twenty are coming.

B But when are they coming?

A Next Monday.

B But I need them this Monday.

2 🔘 Listen and check your answers.

3 Practise reading the dialogue again.

Role-play

1 In pairs, role-play conversations about problems.

Student A
You are the customer. Look at File 16 on page 89.

Student B
You are the supplier. Look at File 37 on page 95.

2 Change roles.

Student A
You are the supplier. Look at File 17 on page 89.

Student B
You are the customer. Look at File 38 on page 95.

10A Bad payers

Listening

1 Read this profile of Peter's English friend Jack Beale.

> Jack Beale runs a gift shop in London called Gifts Galore. Peter <u>first</u> met him in a pub <u>soon after</u> Teresa and Peter arrived in London, and they became friends immediately.
>
> When Peter started up Present Time with Teresa, Jack gave him quite a lot of helpful advice. In return Jack has sometimes used his connection with the Perfect Partners to get big discounts for bulk buying.
>
> Jack is a very energetic person and has lots of bright ideas, but he doesn't always pay his bills on time.

  a What are Jack's strengths? … and his weaknesses?
  b Is he a good person to do business with?

2 Read the profile again and underline all the time expressions. The first two have been done for you.

3 Complete these sentences with these words:

> after   immediately   on time   first

  a Teresa _____ met Peter in L'Aquila.
  b They liked each other _____ .
  c Teresa always gets to the shop _____ , but Peter often arrives late.
  d Soon _____ they opened the shop, Teresa began to feel really happy in her new life.

4 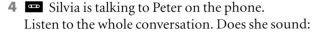 Silvia is talking to Peter on the phone. Listen to the whole conversation. Does she sound:

  a angry? **b** amused? **c** sympathetic?

5 Listen again. Choose the correct answer to the questions below.

  a Who has received a letter from the supplier?
    – Jack
    – Silvia
    – Silvia and Peter

  b Why is it mainly Peter's problem?
    – Peter is in London.
    – Peter is expert in legal matters.
    – Jack is Peter's friend.

  c Peter is going to:
    – call Jack
    – write to Jack
    – pay Jack's share of the bill.

  d Why does Silvia say 'What's the matter with your friend?'
    – She thinks Jack may be ill.
    – She is angry and doesn't understand why Jack hasn't paid.
    – She thinks Jack wants to talk about an important topic.

  e What does Silvia mean when she says 'Sort out your friend'?
    – She wants Peter to tell the police about Jack.
    – She wants Peter to talk to Jack and get him to pay.
    – She wants Peter to tell Jack that she is angry.

6 Look at these sentences from the conversation. Do the words in *italics* refer to Jack, Peter, the supplier, the situation, or the group?

    a I'll call *him*.
    b None of *us* can.
    c We had a letter from *them* this morning.
    d Why hasn't *he* paid yet?
    e I don't know anything about *it* yet.
    f I thought *he* was reliable.

Speaking

Peter and Teresa are discussing some of the things they planned to do.

1 ▭ Look at the pages from their personal organizers.

a Listen and put a ✓ next to the things they have done. Put a ✗ next to those they haven't done yet.

b Which tasks do they not mention?

2 Listen again and repeat what they say.

3 Continue in the same way for the rest of their plans.

Student A
You are Peter. Your diary is on the left.

Student B
You are Teresa. Your diary is on the right.

USEFUL LANGUAGE
Have you paid for the T-shirts yet?
Have you … yet?
Yes, I have. I did it yesterday / last week.
Yes, I've already …
No, not yet, but I'm going to do it now / tomorrow …
Oh no, I haven't. Don't worry, I'll do it now.

▶ **future** page 114

Grammar
present perfect with *yet* and *already*

1 Look at these sentences:

Jack Beale hasn't paid yet.
Silvia has already had a letter from Classic T-shirts.
Has Marek had a letter yet?

– Does Silvia think that Jack *will* pay? Which word tells us this?

– Is Peter surprised that Silvia has had a letter so soon? Which word tells us?

– Does Peter expect that Marek will receive a letter too? Which word tells us?

2 Underline the correct word in brackets.

a Tell Marek. Nobody has told him (already / yet).

b But you needn't tell Peter. Teresa has (already / yet) told him.

c And tell the accountant. She doesn't know (already / yet).

d Have you had a letter (already / yet)?

e Silvia has (already / yet) booked her ticket.

▶ **present perfect** page 119

AUGUST

5 MONDAY	Ask bank about loan repayments.
6 TUESDAY	Write to Venezuelan Embassy.
7 WEDNESDAY	Buy flowers for Teresa.
8 THURSDAY	Enquire about Spanish language courses.
9 FRIDAY	Pay for the T-shirts. Fax order for birthday cards.
10 SATURDAY	
11 SUNDAY	

AUGUST

Choose new supplier for toys.	MONDAY 5
	TUESDAY 6
Call Mr Müller in Berlin.	
Find a new cleaner for the shop. Send back broken teapots.	WEDNESDAY 7
Arrange appointment with Chamber of Commerce.	THURSDAY 8
Speak to Isabel about overtime.	FRIDAY 9
	SATURDAY 10
	SUNDAY 11

10B Repeated requests for payment

Reading

1 Read the following statements and say which of them are true or false in your opinion.

  a A letter is a less formal way of requesting payment than a telephone call or personal visit. _____

  b All letters requesting payment should be firm but also as polite as possible. _____

  c Normally you should make it quite clear when you don't trust a customer. _____

2 With difficult customers, it is common practice to send a series of three letters of *increasing strength*.

  a Look at the letters and say in which order you think they were sent. Why?

  b What information is included in all of the letters? (e.g. customer's name)

3 Read these notes about the style of the three letters and find examples in the letters.

> The first letter is usually a simple request for payment. It should include details of the previously agreed payment date (e.g. _____), and set a new time limit (e.g. ²_____). It should mention that copies of relevant invoices / statements are enclosed (e.g. ³_____). It usually asks the customer to ignore the letter if they have already paid (e.g. ⁴_____).
>
> The second letter is a further request for payment and should include a reference to previous correspondence (e.g. ⁵_____). It should remind the customer that payment has not yet been received (e.g. ⁶_____) and, if appropriate, that no reply to the first letter has arrived. It should insist on payment within a certain time (e.g. ⁷_____), and say what action will be taken if this does not happen (e.g. ⁸_____).
>
> The third letter is a final demand and is shorter. It will sometimes threaten legal action (e.g. ⁹_____).

Ⓐ

Our Ref.   LG / 731 / 123
Your Ref.   4Q2 / YT

Dear Mr Brown,

With reference to our letter LG / 731 / 123 if the amount of £531.21 is not received within seven days, we shall refer this matter to our solicitor.

Yours sincerely,

Ⓒ

Our Ref.   LG / 731 / 123
Your Ref.   4Q2 / YT

Dear Mr Brown,

RE: Non-payment of account number 731.

I would like to bring the above item to your attention. The amount of £531.21 relating to our invoice number 123 (a copy of which is enclosed) is now 30 days overdue.

Would you please ensure payment within the next seven days.

Yours sincerely,

Linda Groves

Linda Groves

Note: Please disregard this letter if payment has already been made.

Ⓑ

Our Ref.   LG / 731 / 123
Your Ref.   4Q2 / YT

Dear Mr Brown,

With reference to our letter LG / 731 / 123 dated 19 October, the amount £531.21 on account number 731 is now significantly overdue. If this amount is not forthcoming within the next seven days, we will be unable to provide you with any further services.

Yours sincerely,

---

4 Which of these expressions would be appropriate in a first request for payment and which in a second request?

  a I am writing to say that your account is now overdue

  b I understand that your account still hasn't been cleared.

  c If you cannot pay, we are afraid that we will have to stop supplies immediately.

  d Would you please ensure payment within the next fortnight.

5 Which of the expressions below would not be suitable in a third payment request (final demand)? Why not?

a If you don't pay immediately, we will phone your husband / wife.

b We now insist on immediate payment.

c Pay now or we'll remove the tyres from your car.

d Unless payment is made immediately, you'll be in serious trouble.

e Although I am reluctant to take legal action, your silence leaves me no alternative.

Grammar
future in *if*-clauses

1 Look at these sentences:

If the amount is not received within seven days, we shall refer this matter to our solicitor.

Please disregard this letter if payment has already been made.

If the full amount is not received, we will be unable to provide further services.

– Which tense of the verb is used in the main clause?

– Which tense is used after *if*?

2 Put the verbs in brackets in the correct form.

EXAMPLE
If she (see) him, she (give) him the message.
If she sees him, she will give him the message.

a I (pay) you if he (pay) me.

b If they (contact) us later today, I (phone) you.

c We (be) in touch by phone if we (decide) to accept your offer.

d If she (not come back) today, she (call) you tomorrow.

e He (manage) without you, if you (not be) there.

▶ **future time clauses** page 115
▶ **conditionals** page 113

Dictation

Peter's friend, Jack Beale, used to have a holiday home in Spain, but he sold it to raise some cash.

1 🔲 Listen to an agent for Spanish Holiday Homes dictating a letter to his secretary. Is the letter very hostile?

2 Listen again and complete it.

> Dear Mr Beale,
>
> Regarding your former property at La Plaza San José 12–2°B, there is an outstanding amount of …

Writing

1 You work for Lockitup Masterkey Safe Systems. You sent a consignment of safes to a customer in Australia on 5 January. Payment is usually made within 30 days of receiving the goods. It is now 5 April and you have not received any payment. Your boss has given you the notes below. Write a letter to request payment.

> Customer details
>
> Name: Comfort Hotels
>
> Address: 3 White House Road, Melbourne, Victoria 3034 Australia
>
> Telephone: 00613–857–8713
>
> Fax: 00613–857–8715
>
> Invoice number: 568/97/5PG (payable 2 March)

2 It is now 9 June and you have not had a reply to your letter dated 5 April. Write again.

3 The customer still hasn't paid. It is now 30 July. Write a final demand.

10C Answerphones

Listening

In business, typical reasons for leaving messages on answerphones are:

– to make an enquiry
– to arrange an appointment
– to chase payments
– to give an invitation.

1 ▭ Listen to four messages left on Julia Weston's answerphone.

   a What is the reason for each call? Use the list above.

Caller	Reason	Name	Number
1		*Gary*	
2	*to rearrange a meeting*		
3			*0171–788–8045*
4			

   b Listen to the messages again and complete the table.

2 Sometimes a recorded message will give you instructions and it can be very difficult to get through to a real person.

   a ▭ Listen to this recorded message. What kind of organization is it?

   b Listen again and note down the numbers you should press if you want:

   – information about a course in accounting ＿＿＿
   – information about a course in benchmarking ＿＿＿
   – information about your account ＿＿＿
   – information about accommodation ＿＿＿

Speaking

1 Rearrange the words below to make an answerphone message.

   a most shop original this souvenir is Gifts Galore London's
   b call no one sorry take I'm to here your there's
   c bleep your leave message and name after please the number
   d soon you to as back we'll get possible as
   e Gifts Galore calling for you thank

2 ▭ Listen and check.

3 Practise using these tips for recorded messages in business:

   – Say names slowly and with special emphasis:
     This is the <u>Bruce Jones</u> Professional <u>Sports Shop</u>.

   – Pause after key words:
     Please leave your name (pause), number (pause), and message (pause), when you hear the signal.

4 Practise saying the message in **1** using the tips. Smile as you speak!

Pronunciation

It is not always easy to differentiate clearly between long and short vowel sounds.

1 ▭ Listen to a recorded message on a theatre answerphone.

   a Which of these words do you hear:
   fool or *full*?
   seats or *sits*?
   pat or *part*?

   b Practise saying the message yourself.

2 ▭ Now listen to the sentences, and say which word in each pair you hear:

   a *heat* or *hit*   **d** *had* or *hard*
   b *chat* or *chart*   **e** *bead* or *bid*
   c *Luke* or *look*   **f** *pool* or *pull*

Role-play

1 Write messages for these situations:

   a You work for a company which organizes different types of holidays. The office is not open on Saturdays but you will send brochures to callers who leave their name, address, and say what type of holiday they are interested in.

   b Your boss has been called away unexpectedly. Give his mobile phone number for really urgent problems – otherwise he'll call back a.s.a.p. if people leave a message.

   c Your offices are closed for the summer break. They open again on 20 August. Apologize for the inconvenience.

   For each message:
   – say who you are
   – explain the situation
   – give instructions.

2 Work in pairs.

   Student A
   Say your first recorded message aloud to Student B.

   Student B
   Listen, then leave a message:
   – saying who you are
   – explaining why you called
   – giving a number where you can be reached.

Student A
Note down what Student B says (as if you were listening to an answerphone message).

3 Reverse roles and continue with Student B's first recorded message.

Student B
Say your first message.

Student A
Listen then leave a message as in **2**.

Student B
Note down what Student A says.

4 Continue with messages **b** and **c**.

11A Wanted

Reading

1 Marek wants to expand his export agency by opening an office in London. Look at the job advertisements. Which one do you think he places?

(A)

Part-time Bookkeeper

One of the UK's leading market research companies is looking for a part-time bookkeeper for 15–20 hours per week. Ideal person should have a degree, experience in all aspects of accounting, and be computer literate.

Flexible hours. Salary based on experience. Please send CV and hand-written covering letter stating availability and current salary to:

Company Administrator,
Johnson Research Agency PLC,
12 Duke Arcade, Kingston Road,
Kingston, Surrey

(B)

High Profile Sales Person (25+)

- Warm personality
- Flexible working approach
- Perfect manners
- Good education
- Excellent references
- Experience in selling accessories useful

Hand-written applications with accompanying CV & photo to:

Decart Accessories, 117 Essex St., London, SW4 7AX

2 Which of these people would be suitable candidates for the three jobs advertised? Explain why.

a Richard:
- likes elegant living
- worked on cruise ship: very popular
- captain of local football team.

b Anna:
- speaks French and Polish
- works as PA to a sales manager
- just finished MS Office course.

c Jane:
- has a young family
- worked in a city bank
- experience of various word processing packages.

3 Find the abbreviations used for the following:

EXAMPLE
curriculum vitae: CV

a United Kingdom
b per annum
c street
d personal assistant
e Microsoft
f twenty-five years old or over
g public limited company

(C)

New fast-growing London-based European import-export agency needs PA.

Self Starter?
£18,000 p.a.

- ► Fluent foreign language(s) essential; Polish an advantage.
- ► Experience in running an office.
- ► Must be friendly & non-smoker.
- ► May involve travel.
- ► A pleasant manner.
- ► Excellent knowledge of MS Office.

Impex Europe PLC, Clifton Place, London, W5 3GL

Listening

1 Which of these questions do you think Marek asks candidates for the job of PA?

a Can you drive?
b Are you good with children?
c Are you good at organizing an office?
d Have you ever prepared displays for shop windows?
e Are you happy to speak on the phone?
f Do you smoke?
g What software have you used?
h Why do you want this job?
i What languages can you speak?
j Why do you want to leave your present job?
k How long have you worked in your present job?
l What is your attitude to fast food chains?
m How would you describe your personality?
n What do other people say about you?
o How long have you lived in London?

2 🔊 Listen to four candidates each answering one of Marek's questions. After each answer, say which question they are answering.

1 ____   3 ____
2 ____   4 ____

Grammar
present perfect with *for* and *since*

1 Look at these sentences:

Anna has worked for her present employer for five months.

She has worked for them since the beginning of January.

– When did Anna start her present job?
– Is she still doing the job?
– Which words tell us when she started her present job?
– Is *for* used to refer to a period of time or to a point in time?

2 Complete these sentences with *for* or *since*.

EXAMPLE
*We have known him **for** ten years.*

a I have used MS Office _____ a long time.
b Teresa has used it _____ last year.
c Silvia has had a shop _____ her parents died.
d Marek has worked full-time in England _____ a few months.

3 Put the verb in brackets in the correct form.

EXAMPLE
How long (live) here?
How long have you lived here?

a How long (study) English?
b How long (know) your best friend?
c How long (be) interested in commerce?
d How long (be) in this school?

4 Now answer the questions.

EXAMPLE
I've lived here for ten years / since I was born.

▶ **present perfect** page 119

Role-play

In groups interview each other for jobs.

Student A
You are the interviewer. Prepare a list of questions.

Student B
You are the candidate. Write down your qualifications and experience on a piece of paper, and give it to Student A.

Reading

Marek is reading the applications again to shortlist candidates for a second interview. Here are the CVs of two candidates that he would like to invite to a second interview. Look at them and say:

1 Which presentation is more effective? Look at:
- layout
- font
- order of information.

2 Which of the two candidates:
  a is better at languages?
  b has spent longer abroad?
  c has better academic qualifications?
  d is more experienced with Microsoft Office?

3 Who seems more suitable for the job? Why?

Anna Musgrove

Personal Information

Name	Anna Musgrove	
Address	19 High Street, Ealing, London	
Telephone	0181 759 7596	
Date of Birth	14th November 1977	
Qualifications	A levels in French, English, and Art	1995
	RSA Diploma in Office Management	1997
	Certificate in Microsoft Office (after two-week in-service course)	1999
	Studying for a certificate in commercial French at the Alliance Française	Present
Languages	Polish: bilingual	
	French: fluent	
	Spanish: GCSE (B)	
Work Experience	Au pair in France	1996
	Travel agency	1997
	PA to the Sales Manager in a large sportswear company	1998 – present
Interests	I enjoy travelling and speaking foreign languages.	
	I collect recipes from different parts of Europe.	
	I take part in the London Marathon every year (last year I came 400th).	

Name:	Susan Williams
Address:	10 Palace Street, Guildford, Surrey
Telephone:	(01483) 651300
Date of Birth:	24 March 1979

Qualifications

1999: Certificate in Office practice
1998: I took GCSE French and Spanish
1995: 6 subjects at GCSE

Work Experience

1998 – present:	Selling advertising space by telephone for European journal.
1998:	Six months as a PA.
1997:	One year working in a bar in Spain.
1996:	One year as an au pair in France.

Other Relevant Experience

I speak French fluently and have a very good level of Spanish.

I am an accurate typist and have experience of a few word processing packages.

Interests

Travelling and music (I sing in a band

Writing

1 Complete the letter of application which Anna sent with her CV using these expressions:

a As you can see …
b As you can see from my interests …
c I would like to …
d I am also very interested in …
e Please let me know …
f Your advertisement asks …

2 Decide what things in Susan's CV would be of particular interest to Marek. Then write her letter of application.

3 Prepare a CV for yourself. Use the headings below to help you. You can invent details.

Personal information

Qualifications

Work experience

Languages

Other relevant experience

Interests

Dear Sir / Madam,

1_____ apply for the position advertised in The Evening Standard on 18 November of PA to the Director.

2_____ from my curriculum vitae, I am at present working as PA to the Sales Manager of a large sportswear company, where I have been working for the last three years.

3_____ for a good knowledge of Polish and French. I am bilingual in spoken and written Polish. My mother is Polish and I have visited Poland every year since I was a child. I achieved Grade A in A-level French. I really enjoy using my languages and am at present studying for the French Chamber of Commerce language diploma at the Alliance Française in London.

4_____ setting up filing systems. This has been a special interest of mine for the last year. Last December I did an in-service course in IT.

5_____, I am a very active person and would be very happy to have the opportunity to work in a small and fast-growing business.

6_____ if you require any further details.

I look forward to hearing from you.

Yours faithfully,

Anna Musgrove

Anna Musgrove

Dictation

1 Listen to the letter Marek sends to Anna inviting her to a second interview. In what order does he mention the following?

a time of the interview
b the job title
c place
d what to bring
e previous contact

2 Listen again and write the letter down.

11C Would Monday be convenient?

Listening

Marek wants to make some changes to his diary.

1 Look at Marek's diary for the week.

   a Which days is he going to be out of the office?

   b Which is his least busy day?

2 🔲 Listen to his conversation with his new PA and complete her notes below.

> **Phone calls:**
>
> - Mr Hix in Birmingham (Tel: ¹_____). Marek is busy. Would Monday be ²_____?
>
> - Mr Gaston (Tel: 543-5670). ³_____ lunch on Thursday. Is ⁴_____ possible for lunch?
>
> - Call Roberta Miller (Tel: 857-3902). Find out when she's ⁵_____ for a meeting. Marek will call to ⁶_____.
>
> - Cancel all other appointments on Friday. Call Teresa. Can she come to Manchester on ⁷_____ to help with the ⁸_____? Marek will pay for the flight.

3 Role-play the phone calls that Anna makes, using her notes.

Student A
You are Anna. Call Mr Hix and Mr Gaston. Look at Marek's diary and make changes where possible / necessary. Note down the changes.

Student B
Look at File 39 on page 95.

USEFUL LANGUAGE
This is Marek Staniuk's personal assistant.
Could you possibly see him before then?
He would be most grateful if you could …
I'm afraid I will be away on …
I won't be able to see you on …
Can he manage another day?
Would Tuesday be convenient?
I'm calling on behalf of …

4 Change roles.

Student A
Look at File 18 on page 89.

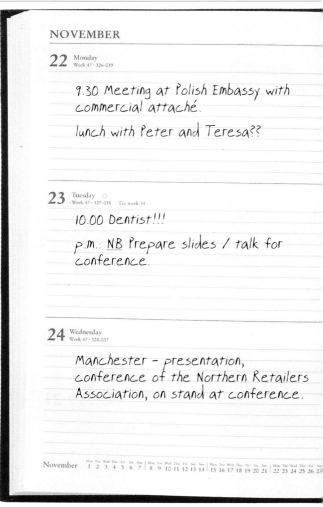

> **NOVEMBER**
>
> **22** Monday
> Week 47 · 326-039
>
> 9.30 Meeting at Polish Embassy with commercial attaché.
>
> lunch with Peter and Teresa??
>
> **23** Tuesday ○
> · Week 47 · 327-038   Tax week 34
>
> 10.00 Dentist!!!
>
> p.m.: NB Prepare slides / talk for conference.
>
> **24** Wednesday
> Week 47 · 328-037
>
> Manchester – presentation, conference of the Northern Retailers Association, on stand at conference.
>
> November 1 2 3 4 5 6 7 | 8 9 10 11 12 13 14 | 15 16 17 18 19 20 21 | 22 23 24 25 26 27

Student B
You are Anna. Call Roberta Miller and Teresa. Look at Marek's diary and make changes where possible / necessary. Note down the changes.

Pronunciation

Numbers and dates can easily be confused on the phone.

1 🔲 Underline the number or date you hear in each line.

   a 13 30 13th   **d** 12 20 20th
   b 17 70 17th   **e** 18 80 80th
   c 15 50 50th

2 Now choose one number from each line in **1** above. Say the number to your partner. Your partner will point to the number he / she hears. Did you say it correctly?

NOVEMBER

Thursday 25
Week 47 · 329–036

11.00 Meeting with Mr Hix (trade fair organizer).
Lunch with manager of toyshop (Mr Gaston).

Friday 26
Week 47 · 330–035

11.00 Meeting with Ann Jones.
(printers)

Saturday 27
Week 47 · 331–034

First Sunday in Advent **Sunday 28**
Week 47 · 332–033

Wed Thu Fri Sat Sun | Mon Tue Wed Thu Fri Sat Sun | Mon Tue Wed Thu Fri Sat Sun | Mon Tue Wed Thu Fri
1 2 3 4 5 | 6 7 8 9 10 11 12 | 13 14 15 16 17 18 19 | 20 21 22 23 24 25 26 | 27 28 29 30 31

Speaking

1 Look at these different ways of referring to dates:

In Britain	In America
In writing 10 June, June 10th 10 / 6 / 99 10 / 6 / 2010	**In writing** 10 June, June 10th 6 / 10 / 99 6 / 10 / 2010
When speaking (on) the tenth of June (on) June the tenth nineteen ninety-nine two thousand and ten	**When speaking** (on) ten June (on) June ten nineteen ninety-nine two thousand ten

2 Practise saying the dates below in British or American English in two ways.

EXAMPLE
8 August 1993:
the eighth of August nineteen ninety-three
August the eighth nineteen ninety-three

a 30 May 1933   c January 1st 1313
b 17 February 2013   d September 4th 2003

3 What's your date of birth?

Role-play

Student A
– You are a secretary to a very busy boss, Mr Johnson.
– He has asked you not to fix any more appointments in the next week.
– Defend him when Student B calls.
– Use the diary in File 19 on page 89 to help you.

Student B
– Your boss wants an appointment with Mr Johnson.
– You know Mr Johnson is in the office on Wednesday.
– Your boss is a good golf player and a member of the same club as Mr Johnson.
– Your boss wants to present his proposal before Mr Johnson goes to meet your competitor in Manchester on Thursday.

USEFUL LANGUAGE
I'm calling to make an appointment …
I'm afraid …
How about …?
Is he free on …
I believe that Mr …

12A Customer complaints

Reading

Read the following article from a retailer's magazine.

1 Which paragraph would the heading *Self Control* best summarize?

2 Which of the words in *italics* mean the following:

   a an opinion
   b a document which can be exchanged for goods
   c a plan or tactic
   d to handle or attend to something
   e a sum of money returned to the customer
   f when you change an item for another item of the same kind

3 🔲 Now listen to Peter dealing with a complaint. Which approach described in the article (1, 2, or 3) does he take?

4 Listen again and answer the following questions.

   a When did the customer buy the mug?
   b What was the problem with the mug?
   c When did the customer discover the problem?
   d What is the outcome?

5 🔲 Now listen to the same situation. This time Teresa deals with the customer's complaint.

   a Which approach (1, 2, or 3) does she take?
   b What is the outcome?

24

Managing Yourself

WHEN A CUSTOMER comes into your shop with a complaint, you can *deal with* it in a number of different ways. You can:

- give a cash *refund*;
- give a *voucher* for the value of the returned goods;
- exchange the goods for something of the same value;
- give a *straight exchange*;
- persuade the customer to wait while you contact the supplier.

When a customer complains, it can be difficult not to take the complaint personally. This can make you behave aggressively, which can then make the customer feel angry. If this happens, a good *strategy* is to count to ten. This allows you to get your anger under control before you speak.

There are three different approaches to dealing with possible conflict with customers:

1 You want to get the customer to accept your *point of view*.
2 You want the customer to be happy.
3 You want to find a solution which satisfies both you and the customer.

The third approach is obviously the most adult and professional, but it doesn't always come naturally. For most people, it requires practice!

Role-play

Role-play the following situation using the third approach in the text.

Student A

You bought a pair of jeans last week. But when you washed them, they lost colour and shrank. They were good quality jeans and you didn't expect to have problems with them. However, you bought them in a sale at a reduced price.

Student B

You are the manager of the shop. The jeans were reduced in your end of season sale. They were regular stock and were not bought in specially for the sale. Your shop has a policy of exchanging faulty goods but not those bought in the sales.

USEFUL LANGUAGE
I'm afraid it's not our policy to …
But I'm telling you …
I bought these in your shop two weeks ago.
I washed them once and …
I'm sorry. We usually …
Would you like to exchange it for …

Grammar
verb + object + infinitive with and without *to*

1 Look at these two sentences:

*You can **persuade** the customer to wait.*
*This can **make** the customer feel angry.*

– What is the form of the verb that follows
persuade? … and *make*?

2 Find these verbs in the article: *get, allow.*

– Are they like *persuade* or *make*?

3 Underline the correct form of the verbs in
brackets.

EXAMPLE
He told her (to wait / wait).

a What will they make me (to do / do)?
b Could you ask them (to come / come) back
   later?
c I'll get him (to call / call) back tomorrow.
d Can you let us (to know / know) as soon as
   possible?
e He persuaded her (to open / open) a
   factory.
f My boss won't allow me (to leave / leave)
   early.

▶ **verb + infinitive with
and without *to*** page 122

Listening

1 Teresa and Peter find that they disagree more and
   more.

a ▣ Listen. What is the cause of their
   disagreement today?

– Peter's friendship with Jack.
– Peter ordered some goods without asking
  Teresa.
– Peter hasn't paid for some goods.

b Does the conversation end in a positive way?

2 Who says the following things? Write *P* for Peter and
   T for Teresa. Then listen again and check your
   answers.

a No wonder customers are complaining. ____
b Do me a favour! ____
c I could go in with Marek. ____
d My heart's not in this any more. ____
e I guess she does. ____

3 Complete these sentences from the dialogue with
   make or *do*. Then listen again to check your answers.

a I want to ____ a job that allows me to be with
   her.
b You can't ____ decisions without asking my
   opinion.

4 Add *make* or *do* to these sentences:

EXAMPLE
It's easy to ____ a mistake.
It's easy to make a mistake.

a I'd like to ____ a course in business
   management.
b Is anyone free to ____ the shopping?
c I like trade fairs because you can meet
   people and ____ new friends.
d We are hoping to ____ a profit.
e What can I ____ to help?
f Who's going to ____ the market research?
g I don't understand this. It doesn't ____
   sense.
h I'm bored. I've got nothing to ____.

▶ *make* and *do* page 115

12B Dealing with complaints

Reading

1 Complete the following letter of complaint with these words:

mentioned	charge	noticed
check	deducted	writing

Dear Mrs Jackson,

I am ¹_____ further to our telephone conversation two weeks ago about invoice no. PX921.

As I ²_____ on the phone, your sales manager, who I met at the Edinburgh trade fair, said that we could have 12% off the gross price of £1,200 for the silk shirts we ordered, and not 8%. However, I ³_____ from the April statement, which arrived this morning, that you have not made the promised adjustment. You also assured us you would not ⁴_____ us for the silk ties which we returned last month, but you have done.

I have, therefore, ⁵_____ £240 (for the silk ties) plus £48 (extra 4% discount) from the April statement and I am enclosing a draft for £1,056 instead of £1,344. Will you please ⁶_____ this and confirm that it is correct?

Yours sincerely,

Gordon Jones

Gordon Jones

2 Find technical words or expressions in the letter above that mean:

a a request for payment

b list showing amounts of money received and / or to be paid

c full price of something before deductions are made

3 How much discount was promised? How much was given? Who promised the higher discount?

4 Why does the writer not want to pay for the silk ties?

Grammar
who and *which*

1 Look at these sentences:

John, who works in films, lives near Hollywood.

We offer an exclusive range of services, which have proved extremely popular.

– Are the above sentences still complete if the *who / which* clauses are removed?

– What form of punctuation is used to show that the *who / which* clause gives extra information?

– In the examples above, when are *which* and *who* used? To talk about a *person* or a *thing*? Find another example in the letter above.

2 Complete these sentences with *who* or *which*:

EXAMPLE

That is our new sales manager, <u>who</u> comes from Spain.

a The new manager, _____ was at the meeting, is from Hungary.

b We are promoting many new designs, _____ will all be available from next week.

c We have agents all over the world, _____ can help you with any problems.

d This is our latest catalogue, _____ describes all our products.

e This software, _____ was expensive to develop, has made them a fortune.

▶ relative clauses with *who* and *which* page 121

Reading

1 In replies to letters of complaint, in what order would you do the following?

a Say what action you have taken, or wish to take, following your investigation. If appropriate, either apologize or reject the complaint.
b Close on a positive note.
c Thank the customer for the letter.
d Explain what you have done, or wish to do, to investigate the complaint.

2 Below are eight paragraphs from two replies, one of which was written in reply to the letter opposite. Find the two first paragraphs. What were the complaints about?

a I can confirm that your account is now up to date. We look forward to receiving your next order.
b As requested, the new consignment has been sent by express delivery this afternoon. Please accept our apologies for any inconvenience.
c Thank you for your fax letting us know immediately that we delivered the wrong items to you this morning (order number T7789 for spare parts for washing machines).
d I have now made the necessary corrections. I do apologize for any inconvenience caused. Mistakes like this do not happen often but are always annoying when they do.
e I have checked both the items on your statement, and it appears that a mistake was made by our accounts department.
f Our sales manager has asked me to say that this is the first time a mistake like this has happened and that he looks forward to meeting you on his next trip to the north of England.
g Thank you for your letter of 10 May, enclosing a draft for £1,056 and pointing out two errors in your April statement.
h On checking the situation, I found that two consignments had been mixed up. I have just been in touch with the other company.

3 Now find the paragraphs to complete each letter and copy the two letters.

Dictation

1 🔊 Listen to someone dictating the reply to a letter of complaint below. Underline the parts that are different or where words are missing.

> Dear Mr Fehr,
>
> Thank you for informing us about the damage done to all the goods we sent you on 9 June (order no. 2981).
>
> We appreciate the problems this has caused you, but we hope we can find a solution as soon as possible.
>
> Could you please return the whole consignment to us so that we can inspect the damage for insurance purposes?
>
> We will dispatch a new consignment immediately. Fortunately, we have everything you need in stock.
>
> Yours sincerely,

2 Listen again and note down the changes. Then write the new letter.

Writing

These are your notes about a letter of complaint you received. Write a reply to the customer, using the structure in the letters above and the information below.

Order no.: ST34

Delivery date: 30 March

Problem: Customer ordered 30 green men's swimming-costumes and 50 black ones. They received 20 green men's swimming-costumes and 50 blue ones.

Reason: Two orders were mixed up.

Solution: Ask customer to return 50 blue costumes at your expense. Offer to send replacements and another 10 green swimming-costumes. Offer a further 2% discount to compensate for inconvenience.

12C Plans

Listening

1 📼 Peter is making plans. Listen to his calls and fill in the table.

	Who he's calling	What the call's about
Call 1		
Call 2		
Call 3		
Call 4		

2 What is Peter going to do?

3 Which calls (1–4) do the following come from?

a How would you like to pay? _____
b Can you confirm the booking in writing? _____
c Can you book me a table? _____
d What are you going to do? _____
e Hello I'd like to … _____
f Can you give me a price for that? _____
g I'm calling about … _____
h Can you arrange for candles and flowers? _____
i Could you give me the card number and expiry date? _____
j I'll call you as soon as it's in. _____
k Can you check if …? _____
l I didn't catch your name. _____

4 Listen and check your answers.

Grammar
(be) going to

1 Look at these sentences:

What are you going to do?
I'm going to take Silvia out for dinner.
Peter isn't going to take the 5 o'clock flight.

– Are the above sentences about things that will definitely happen in the future or are they about Peter's intentions for the future?

– Which words tell us?

– What is the form of the verb after *(be) going to*?

2 Complete these sentences using *(be) going to*:

EXAMPLE
What / Teresa / do in future?
What is Teresa going to do in the future?

a She / not finish the course.
b He / look for a new job.
c she / leave London?
d They / not go.
e What / Peter and Teresa / do with the shop?

▶ **future** page114

Pronunciation

On the phone some words can be easily confused when they are different because of one sound.

1 📼 Listen and underline the word you hear.

a I asked her to cash / catch it.
b Three / free new products for you to try.
c How many chairs / shares do you have?
d There's a buyer / fire in the shop.
e My mouse / mouth isn't working!

2 Listen again and repeat.

3 Say a word from each line in the list below. Your partner will point to the word you say. Is it the same as the one you said?

a thirst   first   **d** bill   fill
b wash   watch   **e** sing   thing
c shoes   choose

Speaking

1 In pairs, role-play conversations using the flow chart below.

Student A
You took a printer to the shop for servicing. You need it back now as you have to prepare some handouts for a sales talk. Phone and ask if it is ready.

Student B
You are the service engineer. Student A calls you.

A	B
say why you are calling	
	ask for spelling of name
spell your name	
	apologize and say the printer isn't ready yet
ask when it will be ready	
	promise to let the caller know
explain that you really need it and why	
	promise to do your best

2 In pairs, role-play another conversation.

Student A
You are the hotel receptionist.
See File 20 on page 89.

Student B
You call a hotel to book a room.
See File 40 on page 95.

3 What do you think Teresa will decide to do?

4 Read these possible endings and choose one.

a Teresa decides to go in with Marek and to promote craft products. The business develops and becomes a well-established agency with a loyal clientele. Teresa and Marek eventually get married.

b Teresa helps Marek to do presentations. She is very good at it. She decides that with these skills, her business experience, and her excellent English she will be able to get a very good job in Italy. She decides to go back.

c Teresa takes out a loan and buys Peter out of the shop. She continues to run it on her own making a small but steady profit from it.

d Teresa sometimes helps Marek. Together they import some handcrafted clocks from Italy which immediately become this year's fashionable craze. They make a small fortune and then Teresa sells the shop and goes in with Marek.

5 Listen to Marek and Peter speaking about Teresa. What do they say about her? Which ending in **4** is most likely?

13A Franchising

Listening

Peter and Silvia are looking into the possibility of franchising.

1 Find words or expressions in the description below that mean:

  a contracts
  b a special name or symbol a company puts on its products to show they produced them
  c the way an organization or individual appears to the public
  d the person who buys into a franchise
  e the person who sells a franchise

> Under franchising agreements a franchisee buys the right to use a franchisor's trade name / trade mark. The franchisor has strict control of the image, the products or service, and of how the business is run.

2 🔲 Listen. Who do you think Peter is talking to? What does he want to know?

3 Listen again. Are the following mentioned as advantages (✓) or disadvantages (✗)?

  a cost _____
  b training _____
  c image _____
  d track record _____
  e administration _____
  f control of the business _____
  g marketing _____
  h sales income _____

4 What advice does Mr Taylor give Peter?

5 🔲 Now listen to Peter and Silvia discussing franchising. What does Peter mean when he says they could *have the best of both worlds*?

  a They could live half the time in Spain and the other half in Britain.
  b They could have their independence but at the same time have help from the franchisor.

6 What disadvantage does Silvia mention?

Grammar
if-clauses and *would*

1 Look at this sentence:

  If Peter had enough money, he would buy a Ferrari. (But he doesn't have enough money.)

– **Is it likely that Peter will buy a Ferrari? Why / Why not?**

– **When we talk about what someone would do in an unlikely situation, what tense is used in the *if-clause*? And in the *main clause*?**

2 Put the verbs in brackets in the correct form.

EXAMPLE
If I (win) a lottery, I (buy) into a fast food franchise.

*If I **won** a lottery, I **would buy** into a fast food franchise.*

  a If I (lose) my wallet, I (go) to the police.
  b If a rich uncle (give) me a lot of money, I (invest) in a hotel.
  c If I (can go) anywhere today, I (fly) to Australia.
  d If I (wake) up one morning and (find) I (be) rich, I (travel) around the world and then I (open) a music megastore.

3 Complete these sentences in two different ways:

  a If I bought into a franchise, I would be able to …
  b If I could have any job, I would be a …
  c If I had responsibility for spending £100 million in my community, I would spend it on …

▶ **conditionals** page 113

Reading

Many franchises are offered on the Internet.

1 Find words in the extract below that mean:

a people who buy your products
b products with our own name
c big variety
d particular types of items sold by a company

2 Now look at more information about Bresler's franchise. Then, in your own words, say what these numbers below refer to.

EXAMPLE
$125,000
$125,000 refers to the minimum total investment.

a $225,000   **c** 10   **e** 1963
b 1930   **d** 7   **f** $15,000

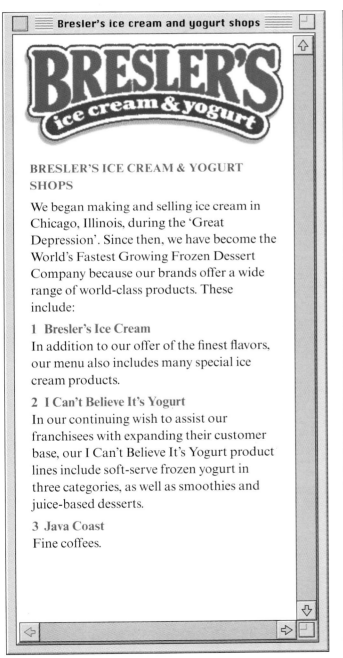

BRESLER'S ICE CREAM & YOGURT SHOPS

We began making and selling ice cream in Chicago, Illinois, during the 'Great Depression'. Since then, we have become the World's Fastest Growing Frozen Dessert Company because our brands offer a wide range of world-class products. These include:

1 Bresler's Ice Cream
In addition to our offer of the finest flavors, our menu also includes many special ice cream products.

2 I Can't Believe It's Yogurt
In our continuing wish to assist our franchisees with expanding their customer base, our I Can't Believe It's Yogurt product lines include soft-serve frozen yogurt in three categories, as well as smoothies and juice-based desserts.

3 Java Coast
Fine coffees.

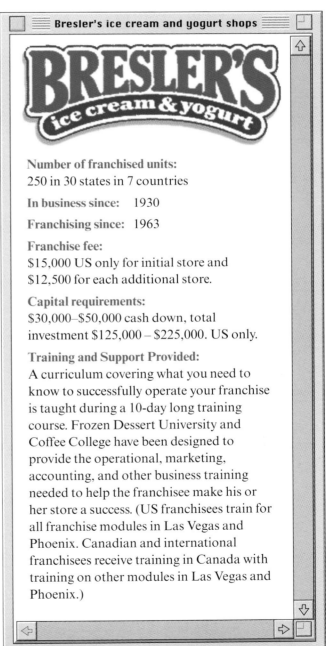

Number of franchised units:
250 in 30 states in 7 countries

In business since: 1930

Franchising since: 1963

Franchise fee:
$15,000 US only for initial store and $12,500 for each additional store.

Capital requirements:
$30,000–$50,000 cash down, total investment $125,000 – $225,000. US only.

Training and Support Provided:
A curriculum covering what you need to know to successfully operate your franchise is taught during a 10-day long training course. Frozen Dessert University and Coffee College have been designed to provide the operational, marketing, accounting, and other business training needed to help the franchisee make his or her store a success. (US franchisees train for all franchise modules in Las Vegas and Phoenix. Canadian and international franchisees receive training in Canada with training on other modules in Las Vegas and Phoenix.)

Reading

Marek is writing to a potential supplier.

1 Complete Marek's offer with these words. Use each word once only.

alternatively	however	but	and
which	furthermore	even if	
because	as	as	

▶ **conjunctions** page 113

2 Read the letter again.

a Which option does Mr Silvestrini prefer?
b Which option do you think Marek prefers? Why?

3 Find the words in column **A** in the letter, then match the items in columns **A** and **B**.

A	B
1 bear the cost of	a for you to look at
2 promote	b for every clock
3 set up	c sample
4 per unit	d promise
5 undertake	e arrange
6 option	f pay for
7 draft	g choice
8 initial	h said
9 indicated	i first
10 for your perusal	j try to sell more of

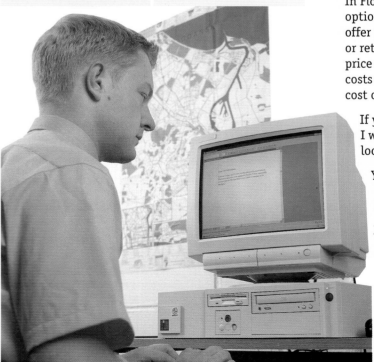

Dear Mr Silvestrini,

Teresa Volpe and I were really pleased to meet you in Florence and see your splendid clocks. I was especially excited about the fact that every clock has a unique design, 1_____ I am sure that this will prove a very strong selling point.

2_____ I explained in Florence, I have an agency in London 3_____ I promote gifts 4_____ are individually made for the gift shop trade. I am looking for products like yours and I am sure that with my contacts I could sell at least 120 units a year.

5_____ we discussed in Florence, we could set up an initial twelve-month agreement between us. There are two ways of doing this:

A
By sale or return. You would send me an initial lot of 30 clocks. I would pay you at the end of the month for any clocks I have sold, and you would send replacements. At the end of twelve months, any unsold clocks would be returned to you.

B
6_____, you would send me a consignment of 30 clocks every quarter and I would pay you at the end of every quarter for any clocks that have been sold. 7_____, I would undertake to pay you for all the clocks you send me at the end of the twelve months 8_____ they have not all been sold.

In Florence you indicated that you might prefer option B. This agreement would mean that I could offer you £50 per unit, delivery CIF*. 9_____ in a sale or return agreement, I would be able to offer you a price of £58 per unit. You would still bear all the costs of transport to London 10_____ I would bear the cost of transport for any returned clocks.

If you could confirm which option you prefer, I will draw up a draft contract for your perusal. I look forward to hearing from you soon.

Yours sincerely,

Marek Staniuk

Marek Staniuk

*CIF: cost, freight, and insurance

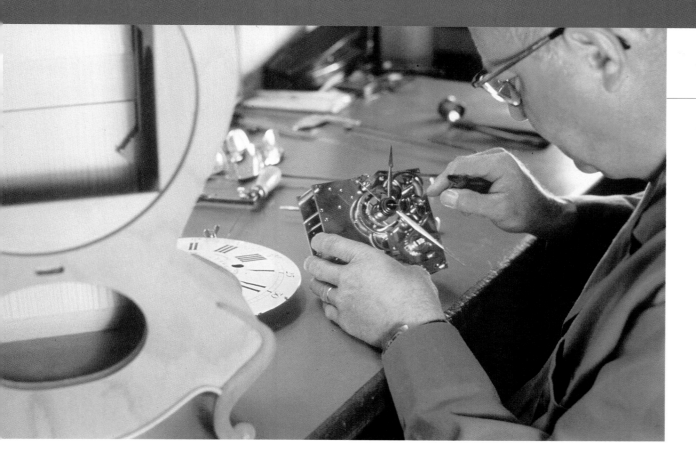

4 Match these different types of sale with the definitions below.

a sale as seen
b sale by description
c sale by sample
d sale or return

1 Goods not seen but sold on the understanding that a true description of their quality and condition is given in the contract of sale.
2 A system where the supplier agrees to take back any goods that a shop has failed to sell. Only the goods that have been sold are paid for.
3 Goods sold on the understanding that they match the quality and condition of a specimen available for inspection.
4 The sale of goods that have been inspected by the buyer. There is no guarantee of quality or condition by the seller.

Dictation

1 Listen to Mr Silvestrini's reply to Marek's offer.

a Does he now prefer option A or B?
b How many clocks does he want to dispatch initially?

2 Listen to the reply again and write it down.

Writing

Write a letter in four paragraphs from Marek to the owner of a shop in Texas who is interested in doing business with his agency.

Address	Mr Frank Bogart, Ideas, #159, North Park Street, Dallas, Texas, USA.
Paragraph 1	Mention the meeting: at a trade fair in Amsterdam last month.
Paragraph 2	Enclose a catalogue of the products you export and refer him to pages 12–14 showing products which might interest him.
Paragraph 3	Explain your terms: Sale by sample Delivery: ex-works Minimum order: 100 units.
Paragraph 4	Say you look forward to doing business together.

13C On the board

Reading

How to play Commercial Snakes and Ladders

First complete the rules with these words:

wait	remember	throw	begin
answer	land	win	do

- Play in two teams (**A** and **B**), or in pairs.
- Each team has a different counter and a list of questions in a file.

  Team A
  see File 21 on page 90.

  Team B
  see File 41 on page 96.

- To ¹_____, you must land on square 40 and answer the question correctly.
- To decide who begins, a player from one team must ²_____ a higher number with the dice than a player from the other team.
- To move forward, you must ³_____ two things:
1 A player from your team must throw the dice.
2 Your team must answer the question on the square where you land.
- If the square you ⁴_____ on is at the bottom of a ladder, go up the ladder and answer the question at the top.
- If you ⁵_____ correctly, throw again.
- If you don't answer correctly, you must ⁶_____ for your next turn.
- However, if you land on a square at the top of a snake, go down it and answer the question at the end.
- If you answer correctly, throw again.
- If you don't answer correctly, you must wait for your next turn.
- If the counter of the other team is on the square where you land, the other team must ⁷_____ again from 0.
- If you begin again, you may have to answer the same questions again, so as you play, ⁸_____ all the answers to all the questions.

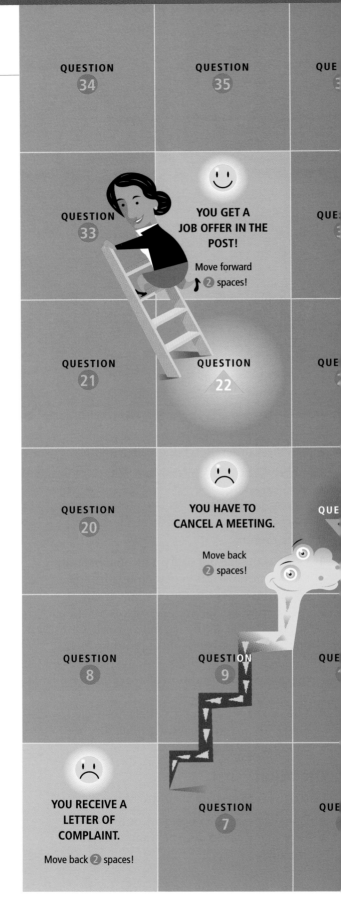

QUESTION 34

QUESTION 35

QUE...

QUESTION 33

YOU GET A JOB OFFER IN THE POST!

Move forward ♪ 2 spaces!

QUE...

QUESTION 21

QUESTION 22

QUE...

QUESTION 20

YOU HAVE TO CANCEL A MEETING.

Move back 2 spaces!

QUE...

QUESTION 8

QUESTION 9

QUE...

YOU RECEIVE A LETTER OF COMPLAINT.

Move back 2 spaces!

QUESTION 7

QUE...

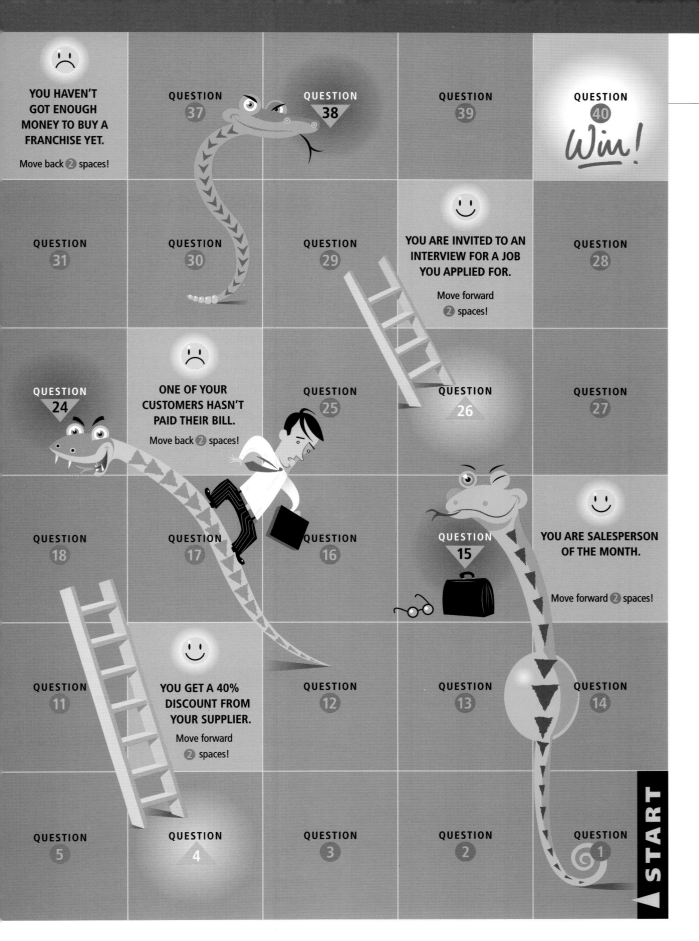

Files Student A

1 Unit 2A page 15

The pie chart is the same as the one on page 15. Student B has different information.

1 Use the questions on page 15 to ask about these age groups:

0–4   5–15   16–24

2 Now answer Student B's questions.

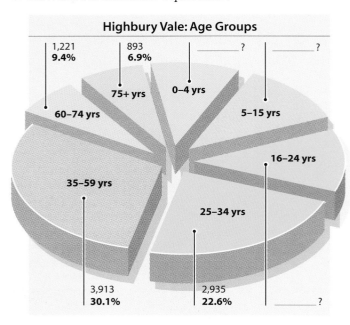

Highbury Vale: Age Groups

1,221
9.4%
60–74 yrs

893
6.9%
75+ yrs

?
0–4 yrs

?
5–15 yrs

16–24 yrs

35–59 yrs

25–34 yrs

3,913
30.1%

2,935
22.6%

?

2 Unit 2C page 19

You are a manager.

– Phone your driver, Student B, to tell him / her that you are coming back from Paris on a different flight.
– You are now coming back the next day, Thursday the 12th.
– Your new flight number is BA 341 and your arrival time at Heathrow, London is 1425.

3 Unit 2C page 19

Student B is coming to see you to sell you some new equipment. He / she phones you because of a change in his / her travel arrangements.

– Make a note of the details of the new flight so that you can meet him / her at the airport.

– You don't understand everything Student B says. When you don't understand something, use the expressions on page 19.

4 Unit 3A page 21

You work in a furniture shop. Student B is a customer. Look at this list to see if you have the things he / she asks you for.

Item	Cost	Number in stock
glass cupboard (with white wood) 1.5m high by 1m wide by 50cm deep	£140 each	2
glass cupboard (with white wood) 1.5m high by 2m wide by 50cm deep	£210	1
glass cupboard (with white wood) 1m high by 2m wide by 50cm deep	£180	1
glass cupboard (with light brown wood) 1m high by 2m wide by 50cm deep	£180	3

5 Unit 3A page 21

You want to buy the items in this list.
Student B is an assistant in an office furniture shop. Ask him / her if he / she has got these items in stock. Use the expressions on page 21.

You want	Dimensions	Number required
white display shelves	2.4m high by 1.5m wide by 30cm deep	3 units
white display shelves	1.5m high by 1m wide by 40cm deep	2 units

6 Unit 4C page 31

1 Call Student B. You want to order four boxes of coloured highlighter pens – pink, yellow, green, and blue. When you call, introduce yourself and say why you are calling. Give Student B these details:

NAME	Natasha
SURNAME	Amadei
COMPANY	Pyramid Data
PHONE NUMBER	0121–465–8989
FAX NUMBER	0121–465–8934

2 Now answer Student B's telephone call and write down the information he / she gives you.

7 Unit 5A page 32

1 Answer Student B's questions using this information:

You are Silvia. Three years ago you left commercial school and you started to manage your parents' shop in Barcelona. You love your work. This is your first trip to England. You have never visited other countries.

You are at the fair for three main reasons:
– you need to find some unusual gifts to sell in your shop
– you need a break
– you hope to meet some interesting people and have some fun. You sometimes find it lonely working by yourself in such a competitive market.

2 Now use the questions on page 32 to ask Teresa about her life.

8 Unit 5A page 32

1 Answer Student B's questions using this information:

You are Peter. You left Australia ten months ago to come to England. In Australia you had a few different jobs. You enjoy having your shop in Highbury and you like living in London. Before you came to England, you went to Italy.

You are at the fair because:
– the shop is very important to you and you want to have a good range of products
– you want to find new products to sell and to get them at the lowest prices
– you would like to talk to other people in the same business. Teresa is not always interested in talking about business.

2 Now use the questions on page 32 to ask Marek about his life.

9 Unit 5C page 37

You are Chris Green. You are a buyer for the toy department of a big department store in London. You left a message for Jo Ford at a company called *Virtuals* to call you back.

When he / she calls you, explain:
– who you are and what you do
– that you saw *Virtuals*' stand at the London Trade Fair
– that you want to buy 2,000 computer games
– that you need all the games immediately
– that you want a 40% discount for this big order.

10 Unit 6C page 43

1 Write a preparation sheet for a call to Terry Coombe at *Picture This*. In January you bought a hundred picture frames.

You would like to:
– buy more picture frames (about 450)
– have a bigger discount.

2 Use your call preparation sheet and call Student B who is Terry Coombe.

3 Now Student B will call you. Use this information to answer his / her enquiry:
– You are John Holmes and you work for the *ABC Trade Fair* in Birmingham.
– Your organization has an agreement with several hotels; they are all fairly expensive.
– You also have the phone number of the local tourist information office which has lists of cheaper bed and breakfast places.

Files Student A

- You don't know exactly how many manufacturers will be exhibiting this year yet. Last year there were ninety-eight.
- There are special seasonal sections – Winter and Summer. There is also a large section for table decorations.

11 Unit 7A page 45

1 Read the first few words to your partner. Then listen to your partner and complete the gap. Continue in this way.

An American went to _____.

They decided to give him one _____.

The children brought them in from the kitchen _____. Their mother smiled and said: '_____, but I don't think they are very tasty.'

2 Check that you and your partner have the same text.

3 Now read your ending:

The American helped himself to a large portion and he put a lot of soy sauce on the special dish. Then he tried it and said: 'You know, it's really very good – it probably only needed some soy sauce.'

4 Now listen to your partner's ending.

5 Which one was more polite?

12 Unit 7C page 49

1 You are staying in the Metropole Hotel, Paris. You are in Paris for a toy trade fair.

Telephone a friend on his / her mobile number. You want to know if he / she is coming to the same trade fair. Use the expressions on page 49.

2 You are having a meeting with an important client who seems interested in your product.

Your mobile phone rings. You really don't want to talk to anyone else at the moment so try to cut the conversation short. Use the expressions on page 49.

13 Unit 8A page 50

You are Silvia. First, there is a list of things you did last Wednesday. This is followed by a list of things that are important to you in your life and work.

1 Read them and prepare to answer the same questions that Peter answered on page 50.

2 Student B will ask you the questions. Answer them.

3 Ask Student B the same questions.

Last Wednesday I ...
- cleaned the carpet (7.30 a.m.).
- opened the shop (8.30 a.m.).
- opened the post (8.45 a.m.).
- chatted to my first customer for fifteen minutes (9.30 a.m.).
- prepared a telephone call to a supplier in Germany – made the call (10.20 a.m.).
- closed the shop for an hour (3.00–4.00 p.m.) to buy some new trainers.
- closed up the shop and did the accounts for the day (7.00–7.30 p.m.).
- went to my English lesson – preparing for an examination (8.00–9.00 p.m.).

Mission Statement
To make a good living to support myself.
To be pleasant and efficient in all my business dealings.
To develop and serve a small and loyal clientele.

14 Unit 8C page 55

1 Call Student B.

You are having problems with your new computer. Call the shop where you bought it.

You need to find out when the technician can come and repair your computer.

You are a little impatient because you really need your computer.

2 Student B was not very helpful in the first call. Call him / her again.

15 Unit 8C page 55

You are a receptionist at a garage which sells new and second-hand cars. One of the mechanics is at lunch. The other mechanic is off sick. They have a lot of work at the moment.

1 When Student B calls, you are not very helpful. You are trying to send an e-mail to your friend while the boss is out.

2 Student B calls you again. You are worried that you might lose customers. Answer the telephone in a helpful and friendly way.

16 Unit 9C page 61

You ordered a hundred karaoke cassettes from *Star Sounds*. When you unpacked the boxes you found the following:

– there were only 85 cassettes
– 23 of the cassette boxes were broken
– 2 of the cassette boxes were empty.

As a result of these problems you have only sixty cassettes to sell.

Telephone the supplier (*Star Sounds*) and explain the situation.

Ask them what they can do to solve the problem.

17 Unit 9C page 61

Your customer calls you because you have sent the wrong order.

Apologize and arrange to send the right goods immediately. Offer to send them by air if it is urgent.

18 Unit 11C page 72

Student B, who is Marek's personal assistant, will call you to rearrange these meetings:

1 You are Roberta Miller. You will be in Australia for two weeks from next Thursday. You wanted to meet Mr Staniuk before you leave. Can he meet on Tuesday or Wednesday?

2 You are Teresa. You are very pleased to be asked to do the presentation. You are free on Wednesday and accept with pleasure. You are a bit surprised that Marek didn't call in person.

19 Unit 11C page 73

This is Mr Johnson's diary.

Monday	All day meeting in Paris.
Tuesday	9.30–11.00 a.m. Meeting, new project.
	12.30–3.30 p.m. Interviews.
	4.00 p.m. Golf.
Wednesday	9.30–11.30 p.m. Factory tour for Swiss visitors.
	Prepare for meeting tomorrow.
Thursday	10.00 a.m. Meeting Manchester – Rolak Associates.
Friday	11.45 a.m. Be at airport, flying to New York 1.00 p.m.

20 Unit 12C page 79

You are the hotel receptionist. Student B calls you. Follow the instructions in this flow chart:

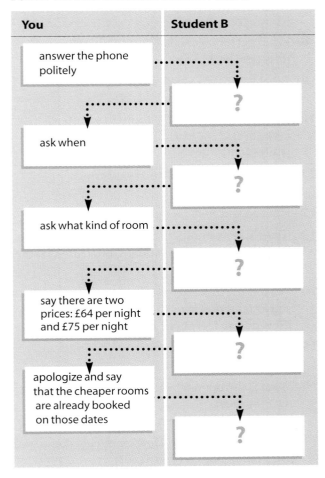

You	Student B
answer the phone politely	?
ask when	?
ask what kind of room	?
say there are two prices: £64 per night and £75 per night	?
apologize and say that the cheaper rooms are already booked on those dates	?

Files Student A

21 Unit 13C page 84

TEAM A

1 At the end of a letter to someone whose name you don't know, what do you write: *Yours ...?*
[**Yours faithfully**]

2 What is the name of a window where goods are displayed at the front of a shop?
[**a shop window**]

3 Is this correct: *I look forward to hear from you?*
[**No, I look forward to hear*ing* from you.**]

4 Is this a suggestion or a request: *Shall we sell the shop?*
[**a suggestion**]

5 Is this correct: *I'm sorry, I don't catch that.*
[**No, I'm sorry, I didn't catch that.**]

6 How do you spell *measurement*?

7 What is another word for a legal agreement that begins with the letter *c*?
[**contract**]

8 What percentage is half of something?
[**fifty per cent**]

9 What is the next word: *long/length; high/ ...?*
[**height**]

10 What is the name of the room in a shop where you keep things?
[**storeroom**]

11 What is the comparative of *expensive*?
[**more expensive**]

12 How do you spell *financial*?

13 Give three examples of leather goods.
[**e.g. wallets, purses, handbags, briefcases, leather jackets, luggage**]

14 What is the missing word in this sentence: *How do you feel this problem?*
[**How do you feel *about* this problem?**]

15 What is the plural of *shelf*?
[**shelves**]

16 What is the missing word in this sentence: *She's away business.*
[**She's away *on* business.**]

17 Correct this sentence: *How much bags do you need?*
[**How *many* bags do you need?**]

18 Does a 'sleeping partner' manage the business?
[**No, he / she only invests money in it.**]

19 Write down this percentage: ninety-three point seven per cent
[**93.7%**]

20 Correct this: *That's a really nice shirt you wear.*
[**That's a really nice shirt you*'re wearing*.**]

21 Complete this sentence: *Documentary credit is a method of ...*
[**payment**]

22 Put this sentence in the passive: *The customer collected the goods.*
[**The goods were collected (by the customer).**]

23 Correct this sentence: *I need some further informations.*
[**I need some further *information*.**]

24 Correct this: *What lovely room!*
[**What *a* lovely room!**]

25 What is the missing word: *I was invited to dinner a colleague.*
[**I was invited to dinner *by* a colleague.**]

26 What word is missing: *I paid £8 this pen.*
[**I paid £8 *for* this pen.**]

27 Correct the verb in this sentence: *My other mobile phone rings.*
[**My other mobile phone *is* ring*ing*.**]

28 What do you call the printed logo and address at the top of a commercial letter: (a) the letterhead; (b) the trade mark, OR (c) the top?
[**The letterhead**]

29 Is this a promise or a request: *I'll send you a fax tomorrow?*
[**a promise**]

30 When you send goods by sea, what is the name of the document you need to fill in: *a Bill of ...?* What is the next word?
[**Lading**]

31 Correct this sentence: *They haven't paid still.*
[**They haven't paid *yet*. / They *still* haven't paid.**]

32 Correct this sentence: *I'm going to doing it this afternoon.*
[***I'm* going to *do* it this afternoon. / I'm *doing* it this afternoon.**]

33 What is the missing word in this sentence: *I'm phoning to ask a quotation.*
[I'm phoning to ask *for* a quotation.]

34 Which sentence is correct? (a) *He gave me some advice.* OR (b)*He gave me some advices.*
[The first one: *advice* is uncountable and can't be plural.]

35 What does PLC stand for?
[public limited company]

36 Correct this sentence: *He asked me help him.*
[He asked me *to* help him.]

37 Which ending is correct: *I've used MS Office <u>since</u> a long time,* OR … <u>*for*</u> *a long time?*
[I've used MS Office *for* a long time.]

38 What is the missing word in this sentence: *Are you good languages?*
[Are you good *at* languages?]

39 Which sentence is correct? (a) *We have to do a decision.* OR (b) *We have to make a decision.*
[We have to make a decision.]

40 How do you spell *accommodation*?

Files Student B

22 Unit 2A page 15

The pie chart is the same as the one on page 15. Student A has different information.

1 Answer Student A's questions.

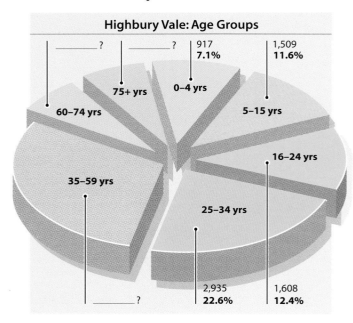

Highbury Vale: Age Groups

- ? 75+ yrs
- ? 0–4 yrs
- 917 / 7.1%
- 1,509 / 11.6% — 5–15 yrs
- 60–74 yrs
- 1,608 / 12.4% — 16–24 yrs
- 35–59 yrs
- ? — 25–34 yrs
- 2,935 / 22.6%

2 Now use the questions on page 15 to ask about these age groups:

35 – 59   60 – 74   75+

23 Unit 2C page 19

You are Student A's driver. Student A is a manager. He / she phones you because of a change in his / her travel arrangements.

- Make a note of all the details about his / her new flight so that you can meet him / her at the airport.
- You don't understand everything Student A says. When you don't understand something, use the expressions on page 19.

24 2C page 19

Your company produces telephone equipment. You are going to Poland to meet a potential customer.

Phone the customer, Student A, to tell him / her that you are arriving on a different flight.

- You are now coming on the same day but four hours later.
- Your new flight number is BA 812 and your arrival time at Warsaw Airport is 1310.

25 Unit 3A page 21

You want to buy the things in the list below. Student A is an assistant in a furniture shop. Ask him / her if he / she has got these things in stock. Use the expressions on page 21.

You want	Dimensions	Number required
glass cupboards with white wood	1.5m high by 1m wide by 50cm deep	3
glass cupboards with white wood	1m high by 2m wide by 50cm deep	2

26 Unit 3A page 21

You work in a shop selling office furniture. Student A is a customer. Look at this list to see if you have the things he / she asks you for.

Item	Cost	Number in stock
display shelf (white) 2.4m high by 2m wide by 30cm deep	£110	2
display shelf (white) 2.4m high by 1m wide by 30cm deep	£60	2
display shelf (grey) 1.5m high by 1m wide by 40cm deep	£50	6
display shelf (white) 1.5m high by 1m wide by 40cm deep	£50	1

27 Unit 4C page 31

1 Answer Student A's telephone call and write down the information he / she gives you.

2 Now call Student A. You want to order one hundred sheets of coloured card – red, green, and yellow. When you call, introduce yourself and say why you are calling. Give Student A these details:

NAME	David
SURNAME	Bronowski
COMPANY	Capitals
PHONE NUMBER	0198–483–2299
FAX NUMBER	0198–483–2678

28 Unit 5A page 32

1 Use the questions on page 32 to ask Silvia about her life.

2 Now answer Student A's questions using this information:

You are Teresa. You came to England ten months ago. Before that you were at school. You love your work but sometimes you find Peter difficult to work with. You have been to France and Spain on holiday.

You are at the fair because:
– Peter thinks you need to get some more exciting ideas for the shop
– you want to meet some new people
– in London you are working in the shop all day and you are ready to have some fun!

29 Unit 5A page 32

1 Use the questions on page 32 to ask Peter about his life.

2 Now answer Student A's questions using this information:

You are Marek. You arrived in England ten days ago. You visited London before you came to the trade fair. You lived and worked in Amsterdam for four years. You went back to Poland three years ago. You enjoy working in your shop there.

You are at the trade fair for three main reasons:
– to investigate a possible market for Polish craft products
– to find some new things to sell in your gift shop in Gdańsk
– to have a good time and make new contacts.

30 Unit 5C page 37

You are Jo Ford. You work in the sales department at *Virtuals*, a supplier of computer games. You have a message to phone Chris Green.

When you call:
– ask to speak to Chris Green and introduce yourself;
– explain that you are returning his / her call;
– find out what he / she wants.

Your maximum discount is usually 35% for orders of 1,000–5,000, but if a customer is very important, you sometimes give a bigger discount for a first order.

Unfortunately, you only have 500 computer games in stock today, and you have promised them to another customer.
– Price each to public: £100.
– Normal price to shops: £75.
– Tomorrow another 10,000 are arriving from China.
– Decide what discount you can offer while talking to Chris Green.

31 Unit 6C page 43

1 Write a preparation sheet for a call to John Holmes, who works for the organizers of a trade fair you want to go to. You need to know:
– where the trade fair is
– about accommodation (the organizers have an agreement with some hotels)
– how many exhibitors there will be
– about the type of sections / products that will be on display.

2 Student A will call you. Use this information to answer his / her enquiry:

You are Terry Coombe at *Picture This*.
– In January your customer ordered 100 picture frames and you gave a special price.
– There could be a further discount if they make a much bigger order – say 500 frames.
– You are not interested in giving a discount for a smaller order.

Files Student B

3 Now use your call preparation sheet and call Student B who is John Holmes, one of the trade fair organizers.

32 **Unit 7A** page 45

1 Listen to your partner and complete the first gap. Then read the next few words to your partner. Continue in this way.

_____ a Chinese family for a dinner. _____ of their special dishes – fish balls. _____ and put them on the table. _____: 'I made these fish balls this morning, _____.'

2 Check that you and your partner have the same text.

3 Listen to your partner's ending.

4 Now read your ending:

So the American helped himself to a large portion and he tasted the special dish. The food was not tasty – he didn't really like it, but he said: 'These are the most delicious fish balls I have ever tasted.'

5 Which ending was more polite?

33 **Unit 7C** page 49

1 You are in Paris for a toy trade fair. You arrived yesterday. You are staying at the Metropole Hotel.

Your friend calls you on your mobile phone. You can't speak to him / her because you are meeting a client at 8 o'clock. It's 8 o'clock now! Use the expressions on page 49.

2 You have nothing to do and you are feeling a bit lonely.

Telephone a friend on his / her mobile. Try to talk for as long as possible. Use the expressions on page 49.

34 **Unit 8A** page 50

You are Marek. First, there is a list of things you did last Wednesday. Below this is a list of things that are important to you in your life and work.

1 Read them and prepare to answer the same questions that Peter answered on page 50.

2 Ask Student A those questions.

3 Student A will ask you the questions. Answer them.

Last Wednesday I ...
- visited a small factory and decided to promote their goods (8.30–12.30 p.m.).
- had lunch with the management in their canteen (12.30–1.30 p.m.).
- took five cases of toys to the airport for export – it took 3 hours to do all the paperwork (2.00 p.m.).
- went back to the shop (5.30 p.m.) and congratulated my assistant on a good day's work.
- recorded the day's takings (5.45–6.30 p.m.).
- wrote out a plan for next day with all the telephone numbers of people I needed to call (6.30–7.00 p.m.).

Mission Statement
To promote Polish products.
To be respected by customers and suppliers as someone who gets things done and is reliable.
To sell interesting things in Poland from all over the world.

35 **Unit 8C** page 55

You work in a computer shop.

The technician is out on a job at the moment and you don't know when he'll be back.

Ten people have called to speak to him this morning.

1 When Student A calls you are not very helpful. You are trying to read the last chapter of your book.

2 Student A calls you again. You are worried that you might lose customers. Answer the telephone in a friendly and helpful way.

1 Call Student A.

Your new car won't start.

Call the garage where you bought it.

You need to find out when the mechanic can come and repair it.

You are a little impatient because you are going on holiday tomorrow.

2 Student A was not very helpful in the first call. Call him / her again.

You work for *Star Sounds*. You are insured against damage to your goods in transit.

One of your customers calls you to make a complaint. Ask your customer to write a formal letter describing the damage. Offer to refund his / her money or to send him / her the missing cassettes and replacement cassettes by air.

You ordered four boxes of white chocolate bars and three boxes of dark chocolate bars. When you opened the boxes you found that:

– 4 of them contained dark chocolate
– 3 of them contained white chocolate
– nearly half of the white chocolate bars were broken.

Call them to explain what has happened.
Ask them what they can do to solve the problem.

Student A, who is Marek's personal assistant, will call you to rearrange these meetings:

1 You are Mr Hix. You arranged a meeting with Marek for Thursday, 25 November at 11 a.m. When you get the call you are a bit annoyed as it's the second time he has rearranged the meeting. You certainly have no intention of going to London to meet Mr Staniuk but you could meet him in Birmingham after 3.30 p.m. He could catch a train to Birmingham from London: they are fast and frequent.

2 You are Mr Gaston. You arranged to have lunch with Marek on Thursday, 25 November. You already have a lunch appointment on Tuesday, 23 November, but you could meet him on Tuesday, 30 November for lunch. You are also free on Tuesday, 23 November in the afternoon.

Student B
You phone a hotel to book a single room for June 8th, 9th, and 10th. You can only afford £64 per night. Follow the instructions in this flow chart:

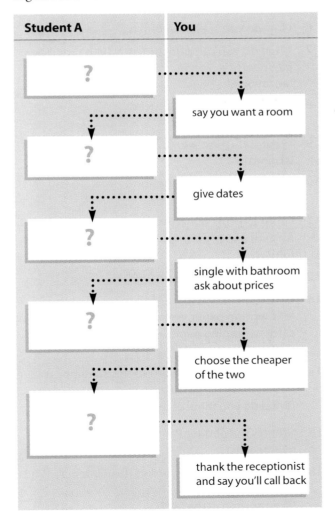

Student A	You
?	say you want a room
?	give dates
?	single with bathroom ask about prices
?	choose the cheaper of the two
?	thank the receptionist and say you'll call back

Files Student B

TEAM B

1 How would you start a letter to someone called Anna Musgrove, if you don't know her?
[**Dear Ms Musgrove**]

2 When you want to buy a ticket for a plane, what is another way to say *reserve*?
[**book**]

3 Is this correct on the phone: *I call back later.*
[**No: I'll call back later.**]

4 Is this a suggestion or a request: *Can you speak more slowly, please?*
[**a request**]

5 How do you ask a caller to wait?
[**Will you hold? / Just a moment. / Hold the line, please.**]

6 How do you spell *responsible*?

7 What do you call a document which requests payment?
[**an invoice**]

8 What does *to purchase* mean?
[**to buy**]

9 What is the next word: *long / length; strong / …*?
[**strength**]

10 When you win a competition, what do you get?
[**a prize**]

11 Complete this sentence with the comparative form of *old*: *My brother is … than I am.*
[**older**]

12 How do you spell *arrangement*?

13 Give three examples of stationery.
[**e.g. writing paper, envelopes, postcards, greeting cards, wrapping paper, diaries, pens, pencils, rubbers**]

14 What is the missing word in this sentence: *What do you think the fair?*
[**What do you think *of* the fair?**]

15 What is the plural of *cupboard*?
[**cupboards**]

16 What is the missing word in this sentence: *Why are you the fair?*
[**Why are you *at* the fair?**]

17 Correct this sentence: *How many money does this cost?*
[**How *much* does this cost?**]

18 A debt is (a) when someone owes you money, or (b) when you owe someone some money?
[**b**]

19 Write down this number: *three thousand, three hundred and thirty-three.*
[**3,333**]

20 Correct this sentence: *What will they do when they will receive the motif?*
[**What will they do when they *receive* the motif?**]

21 Complete this expression to say something costs nothing: *It is …*
[**free (of charge)**]

22 Put this sentence in the passive: *The customer's bank pays for the goods.*
[**The goods are paid for (by the customer's bank).**]

23 Correct this sentence: *I would like place a big order.*
[**I would like *to* place a big order.**]

24 Correct this sentence: *I wrote him letter.*
[**I wrote him *a* letter.**]

25 What is the missing word in this sentence: *I was in Spain business.*
[**I was in Spain *on* business.**]

26 What word is missing: *The operator put me through the manager.*
[**The operator put me through *to* the manager.**]

27 Correct the verb in this sentence: *Hello. Do I disturb you?*
[**Hello. *Am* I disturb*ing* you?**]

28 Is another word for *a shop*: (a) a warehouse, (b) a store, OR (c) a chain?
[**store**]

29 Does this sentence express certainty or possibility: *We must be on the wrong plane.*
[**certainty**]

30 Complete this phrase which you can find printed on a box with things that break easily in it: *Handle with …*
[**care**]

31 Correct this question: *Does Teresa yet know?*

[Does Teresa *know yet*?]

32 Correct this sentence: *I'll phone you if they will contact us.*
[I'll phone you if they *contact* us.]

33 What is the missing word in this sentence: *Can we arrange a time an appointment?*
[Can we arrange a time *for* an appointment?]

34 Which sentence is correct? (a) *The teacher gives them a homework every day.* or (b) *The teacher gives them homework every day.*
[b]

35 What does cv stand for?
[curriculum vitae]

36 Correct this sentence: *It is important to make customers to feel special.*
[… make customers *feel* special.]

37 Which sentence is correct? (a) *I've worked here for the beginning of the year.* or (b) *I've worked here since the beginning of the year.*
[b]

38 What is the missing word in this sentence: *She persuaded him be a designer.*
[She persuaded him *to* be a designer.]

39 Correct this question: *What would you do if you would win the lottery?*
[What would you do if you *won* the lottery?]

40 How do you spell *consignment*?

Tapescript

1A Listening

Exercise 1

MAREK My name is Marek and I'm from Poland. I'm just beginning to work in business, and for me business is about taking risks and working hard – incredibly hard. I hope it is also about making lots of money quickly. I think being lucky is essential. I hope I'll be lucky.

TERESA I'm Teresa and I'm from Italy. I've just left school, so I don't know much about business. I suppose it involves solving a lot of problems. But I like the idea of meeting a lot of new people and having fun.

SILVIA My name is Silvia and I'm from Spain. I've been in business since I was twenty-one. And for me business is basically being very busy. It means always organizing and using every minute of every day, and being polite and efficient. It also means travelling a lot and not seeing your family very much.

PETER I'm Peter from Australia. I think making a good impression is very important in business. You know, looking good, and going out to expensive lunches. I suppose being stressed is a problem for some people – but not if you're young.

1B Listening

Exercise 2

MUM … a shop in London! If you sell it, Peter, there'll be enough money for you to travel around Europe and …

PETER Sell it! You must be joking. No, Mum. This is it! This is my big opportunity! A shop in England. I can open a new shop. I can see it now – 'Pete's Emporium'. I can import things from Australia. Sell the shop! No chance. I want to make a go of it.

MUM It's not a bad idea, Peter. But what about your cousin? Perhaps she wants to sell it.

PETER I can call her.

MUM And Peter, it's very hard work, you know, running a shop. The hours are very long.

PETER Mum, I like hard work. And this is just the beginning, you know. A little shop in London, then a group of shops in Britain, then a chain of shops all around the world. Rome, London, Paris, New York, Tokyo, Sydney … I can be a millionaire if I do this right.

MUM Don't be silly, Peter. Get real! It's a big financial risk. You don't know what you're doing!

PETER Why not, Mum? Millionaires always start with a simple idea.

1C Listening

Exercise 1

TERESA Well, I don't know! What do you think we should sell?

PETER We could sell gifts – you know, little presents and things like that.

TERESA But there are lots of gift shops in London already. I really don't think they need another gift shop.

PETER Yes, but Teresa, think! We could sell different things – things from Australia, things from Italy. There must be a market for original and unusual things.

TERESA What about capital? We'll need a lot of capital.

PETER No, don't forget that Giuseppe left us some money.

TERESA Yes, but I wanted to use that money for a holiday.

PETER Yes, I can understand your feelings, Teresa. But I think we should use the money for the future. I'd like to keep the shop.

TERESA Why don't you come to L'Aquila and we can discuss it?

PETER That's a good idea. Then we could both go to London to meet the lawyer and see the shop before we decide what to do.

1C Speaking

Exercise 1

1 MARIA Can I speak to George, please?
   ISABEL I'm afraid he's not in his office right now.
   MARIA Oh dear. I wanted to speak to him.
   ISABEL Would you like to leave a message?
   MARIA Yes, can you tell him Maria called?

2 MAN I'd like to speak to someone about my bill.
   WOMAN Okay. I'll put you through to Ms James. She's the person who deals with payments.

3 WOMAN Could I speak to Mr Edwards, please?
   MAN I'm sorry. I think you have the wrong number.
   WOMAN What number is it?
   MAN It's 01945–723–723.
   WOMAN Sorry to disturb you.

4 PETER Hello, can I speak to Teresa Volpe, please?
   MOTHER Who's calling, please?
   PETER It's Peter, from Australia.
   MOTHER Oh hello, Peter. Just a moment, please. Teresa!
   TERESA Hello?
   PETER Hello, Teresa?
   TERESA Speaking.

1C Pronunciation

Exercise 1

mistake   wanted

Exercise 2

disturb   payment
address   message
decide   office
idea   number
discuss   speaking

2A Reading

Exercise 5

PETER I really like L'Aquila, you know, Teresa. I didn't know what to expect but I really like it, especially all the old medieval buildings. You know, we don't have those in Australia. Then the other really good thing is the safe streets. There really is very little crime on the streets.

TERESA That's true. What else do you like?

PETER Well, I think the town centre's very nice, and all the shop windows always look good.

TERESA Well, I can't wait to go to London.

PETER You've never been there?

TERESA Just once, on a school trip. We had a day in London.

PETER What do you remember about it?

TERESA I remember black taxis and red buses, then lots of music shops with millions of records and CDs. I remember the big green parks in the centre of the city. And I remember all the busy city streets and the night clubs and the hamburger bars everywhere.

2A Speaking

Exercise 1

a seven hundred
b three thousand
c three thousand seven hundred and fifty
d thirty-five point eight per cent
e three hundred and one
f seven thousand three hundred
g eight thousand three hundred and fifty-one
h seventy-five point five two per cent

2B Dictation

TERESA I'd like to send a letter to your mother's friend in London.

PETER That's a good idea. What do you want to say?

TERESA Well, 'Thank you for inviting us' … and I'd like to ask her if she'd like anything particular from Italy.

PETER Okay, I'll help you.

TERESA 'Dear Mrs Bolton' … or should I use her name, 'Mary'?

PETER No, you don't know her. Mrs Bolton is best.

TERESA Okay. 'Dear Mrs Bolton', comma, 'Thank you very much for inviting me // to your house.' // Is that okay?

PETER 'Thank you very much for inviting me to your house.' Yes, that's fine. '…with my cousin Peter.'

TERESA Yes, 'with my cousin Peter', full stop. But I want to say something else to say 'thank you'.

PETER How about: 'It really is very kind of you'?

TERESA Yes, that's great. Thanks. 'It really is very kind of you,' full stop. // New paragraph: 'I'd like to bring you a present.' // 'I'd like to bring you a present.'

PETER Ask her if she likes olive oil. My mum always gets Italian olive oil.

TERESA Oh, okay … 'Do you like olive oil?' How do you spell 'olive oil'?

PETER O–L–I–V–E: olive; oil: O–I–L.

TERESA Right. 'Do you like olive oil?', question mark.

PETER That's fine. She'll like that.

TERESA How shall I finish?

PETER How about: 'Looking forward to meeting you soon. Best wishes, Teresa.'?

TERESA 'Looking forward to meeting you soon. Best wishes, Teresa.' I think I'll put 'Teresa Volpe'. She doesn't know me.

PETER Yes, that's better.

TERESA So that's: 'Dear Mrs Bolton. Thank you very much for inviting me to your house with my cousin Peter. It really is very kind of you. I'd like to bring you a present. Do you like olive oil? Looking forward to meeting you soon. Best wishes, Teresa Volpe.'

2C Listening

Exercise 1

MRS BOLTON Hello?

PETER Hello. Can I speak to Mrs Bolton, please?

MRS BOLTON Speaking.

PETER This is Peter Clapton calling from Italy. How are

Tapescript

you, Mrs Bolton?

MRS BOLTON I'm fine, thanks. And you? Are you excited about coming to London?

PETER Yeah, and I'm very excited about seeing the shop. Actually, I'm phoning to say that our flight has been changed. We're coming on a different flight.

MRS BOLTON I'm sorry, I didn't catch that.

PETER I said we're coming on a different flight. We're now coming on the next day, on Friday the eighteenth. Our new flight number is AZ 564. We're arriving at two o'clock in the afternoon your time.

MRS BOLTON So, that's Friday the eighteenth and your flight number is AZ 564. You're arriving at two o'clock in the afternoon our time.

PETER That's right. Is that a problem for you?

MRS BOLTON No, that's fine. See you soon.

2C Pronunciation

Exercise 1
EXAMPLE
I'm coming on a different flight.

a My flight's been changed.
b He's coming on a different flight.
c I'd like to see you tomorrow.
d I've finished.
e They're arriving at three o'clock.

3A Listening

Exercise 3
PETER Let's take the measurements. Have you got a tape measure?

TERESA Yes, I have.

PETER Okay, let's start with the walls. How long is this wall?

TERESA Hold the end of the tape measure. Let me see, that's five metres and fifty centimetres.

PETER Did you say fifty or fifteen?

TERESA Fifty, five oh.

PETER Okay, so that's length – five metres fifty. Now let's measure the height.

TERESA Okay, but I need a chair to stand on.

PETER Can you read it now? How high is it?

TERESA Three metres twenty.

PETER Height – three metres twenty. Let's do the width of the door now.

TERESA Just a minute, let's see … that's one metre ten wide.

PETER So that's …

3B Dictation

MONICA 'Dear Mr Jordan.'

SECRETARY Is that J–O–R–D–A–N?

MONICA Yes, that's right. So: 'I am writing to say // that the baseball bats // you sent us yesterday // were the wrong ones.' // Got that?

SECRETARY Yes, carry on.

MONICA 'We asked for size two, for children, // not size one for adults. // Last week the problem was the wrong caps, // this week it is the wrong bats.' //

SECRETARY Fine.

MONICA New paragraph. 'Please send us some new bats immediately', colon, // 'fifteen small ones,' comma, // 'as ordered on August thirteenth.' // Okay?

SECRETARY Yes. 'Yours sincerely, Monica Taylor'.

MONICA Thanks. Could you just read it back to me to see how it sounds?

SECRETARY Sure: 'Dear Mr Jordan, I am writing to say that the baseball bats you sent us yesterday were the wrong ones …'

3C Listening

Exercise 1
OPERATOR Good morning. Australian High Commission.

PETER I'd like to speak to the Trade Commissioner, please.

OPERATOR I'm afraid the line's engaged. Will you hold?

PETER Yes, I'll hold.

OPERATOR The line's free now. I'm putting you through.

SECRETARY Trade Commissioner's office. How can I help you?

PETER I'd like to speak to Mr Cody, please.

SECRETARY Who's calling, please?

PETER My name is Peter Clapton.

SECRETARY I'm afraid the Trade Commissioner is in a meeting at the moment. Can you call back this afternoon?

PETER Okay, I'll call back at about four o'clock.

SECRETARY Goodbye. I'll tell him you called.

3C Pronunciation

Exercise 1
EXAMPLE
Are you busy?

a What's your name?

b Will you hold?

c Who's calling, please?

d Is he free this afternoon?

e Will you call back later?

f Are you free next week?

g When are you free?

h How can I help you?

i What would you like to know?

4A Listening

Exercise 1

1 PETER Look at these. They're three-dimensional. Touch them, see? They're not flat.

TERESA Let's ask about the price. Excuse me. Can you give us a price for these T-shirts, please?

STALL HOLDER Sure, these are eleven pounds each.

TERESA Is there a price for bulk orders?

STALL HOLDER Sure. They cost a hundred pounds for ten … that's a ten per cent discount.

TERESA Thanks.

2 PETER Do you think we should get any of these?

TERESA No, we want classy things in the shop.

PETER Yes, and unusual things. You can get these on any street corner in London.

STALL HOLDER These are the best London T-shirts you'll find, sir. With respect, only the best shops sell our T-shirts.

PETER Yes, but they're not really what we're looking for. How much are they anyway?

STALL HOLDER We sell them in packs of ten. They'll cost you thirty pounds a pack, three pounds per shirt, but you can sell them for seven pounds ninety-nine. That's a good profit.

TERESA Okay well, we'll think about it. Thank you.

3 TERESA Look at these! That's a strange combination – philosophy and football.

PETER They're quite interesting though.

TERESA I wonder how much they are. Excuse me. Can you give me a price for these T-shirts, please? They're very original.

STALL HOLDER Certainly. We sell these at a hundred and sixty-nine pounds ninety for ten.

PETER So that's a unit price of …

STALL HOLDER Sixteen pounds ninety-nine.

PETER That's quite expensive.

STALL HOLDER Yes, I know but they're original and very good quality. People really like them.

4C Listening

Exercise 1

A Hello? Hello? This is Mr Peters speaking from the Bucksleigh Community School. That's B–U–C–K–S–L–E–I–G–H Community School. Could you send us some staplers, standard size, and scissors please. Twenty staplers and twenty-five pairs of paper scissors. Thank you.

B Hello. This is Mrs Davis of Slough Enterprises PLC. That's S–L–O–U–G–H Enterprises PLC. We need some files and paper clips. The files are blue A4, your code: A4, 32, X, and we need sixty, six oh. And you'd better send twenty packets of paper clips.

C Hello. This is Jean Turner from Curtis Consultancies, Ltd. That's C–U–R–T–I–S. Thank you for your last delivery. It arrived this morning. I'm afraid there were a few things you forgot. You sent us plenty of red and black Biros, but no blue ones. Can you send us seventy blue Biros. You didn't send us any ink rubbers. We need fifteen boxes a.s.a.p. please. Thanks.

4C Pronunciation

Exercise 2

a make	**f** leather	**k** new
b paper	**g** files	**l** true
c keep	**h** buy	**m** staff
d free	**i** phone	**n** ask
e yes	**j** go	

5A Listening

Exercise 3

PETER I saw you this morning at the T-shirt stand. Did you order any?

SILVIA Oh, yes, the tourist T-shirt stand. Yes, I did. I ordered a lot. They're very nice T-shirts.

PETER Yes, they're very nice and not too expensive.

SILVIA Yes, I know.

PETER Is this the first time you've been to this fair?

SILVIA Yes, it is. I've been to a lot of fairs in Spain but this is the first time I've been to Birmingham. What do you think of the fair?

PETER It's really exciting. In fact, it's the first fair I've been to. I'm just beginning. You see, I inherited a shop in London and decided to open it up again as a gift shop.

Tapescript

SILVIA That's great.

PETER Can I get you a drink? It's very hot in here.

SILVIA Thanks. I'd like that.

Exercise 4

TERESA Hey, that's a really nice shirt you're wearing. I really like it. Where did you get it? I'd like to sell shirts like that.

MAREK Why? Do you have a clothes shop?

TERESA Oh, no, no, a gift shop, actually. But we could sell a few unusual shirts. What about you? Are you here to sell or to buy?

MAREK A bit of both, actually. I'm from Poland and I'm interested in selling Polish craft products. I have a small export agency but I also have a little gift shop in Gdańsk.

TERESA Have you found any interesting products here?

MAREK I think so, I like some of the T-shirt ideas – especially the Philosophy Football.

TERESA Oh, do you like football?

MAREK Like football? I live for football! But you're not English. Where are you from?

TERESA I'm from Italy.

MAREK So what are you doing here?

TERESA Well, it's a long story …

Exercise 5

PETER Teresa, I'd like you to meet Silvia. She has a very successful gift shop in Barcelona.

TERESA Pleased to meet you, Silvia.

SILVIA Nice to meet you.

PETER She has some fantastic ideas.

5B Dictation

MANAGER 'Dear Mr Anderson,' A–N–D–E–R–S–O–N. 'Thank you for your recent enquiry // about Nicholas,' N–I–C–H–O–L–A–S, 'Jones', that's J–O–N–E–S, // 'the internationally famous Bruce Willis,' that's W–I–L–L–I–S, 'look-alike' full stop.// 'We are pleased to enclose his photograph,' comma, // 'biography,' comma, // 'and press comments', full stop. // New paragraph. 'Please contact us // as early as possible // if you would like to engage him // as he is much in demand', full stop. 'We look forward to hearing from you. Yours sincerely …'

5C Listening

Exercise 1

LIZ Could I speak to Marek Staniuk, please?

MAREK Speaking.

LIZ This is Liz Parker from 'Just for You'. You left a message yesterday. I'm returning your call.

MAREK Oh yes. A group of partners and I are interested in your products.

LIZ Which ones in particular?

MAREK Your gift bags. But we want a forty per cent discount on a bulk order.

LIZ Where are you based? In the UK or abroad?

MAREK One shop's in London, another in Spain, and one in Poland.

LIZ I'm afraid our maximum discount is usually twenty per cent for a single order of a thousand packets to one address.

MAREK Oh dear! The quantity is okay, but we wanted three different addresses.

LIZ I'm afraid I can't offer you more than that.

MAREK Okay. I'll talk to my partners. Bye.

Exercise 3

LIZ Could I speak to Teresa Volpe, please?

TERESA Speaking.

LIZ This is Liz Parker. I'm calling from 'Just for You'. I'm returning your call.

TERESA Oh good. I've just opened a gift shop in London. I saw your stand at the Birmingham trade fair and I thought your gift bags looked lovely. I'm looking for some special gift bags. The problem is the quantity and the discount.

LIZ I'm afraid our maximum discount is usually twenty per cent for a single order of a thousand packets.

TERESA Well, the quantity is fine, because three of us want to order together. But the thing is we already have an offer of a better price from another company, which my partners are prepared to accept.

LIZ Oh.

TERESA Well, I was hoping for a thirty-five per cent discount.

LIZ Oh. Um … how about twenty-five per cent?

TERESA Yes, okay, but only if you can deliver them to three different addresses.

LIZ Well, okay, … as you're just starting.

TERESA Great. We'd like them delivered before next Tuesday, if that's …

5C Pronunciation

Exercise 1

I've just opened a <u>gift</u> shop in <u>London</u>.
I'm looking for some <u>special</u> gift bags.

Exercise 2

a I thought your gift bags looked lovely.
b The problem is the quantity and the discount.
c Three of us want to order together.
d But the thing is, we already have an offer of a better price.
e Well, I was hoping for a thirty-five per cent discount.
f Because we'd like them delivered before next Tuesday.

6A Listening

Exercise 1

PETER   I'm really worried about Christmas because I know it could be our best time. But there's so much competition in London.
SILVIA   Yes, I know. It's always a difficult time for me too.
PETER   The trouble is the competition. It's so difficult to be special and different.
SILVIA   Couldn't we do something together?
PETER   We could decide on a free gift and all order together. That would be cheaper.
SILVIA   Do you mean a calendar or something?
PETER   No, calendars are boring and old-fashioned.
SILVIA   Well, we could order a T-shirt to give to good customers.
PETER   Yes, that's a great idea. Why don't we design our own?
SILVIA   Shall we ask the others what they think?
PETER   Yes, but I think it's a brilliant idea. We could give them to customers who spend more than fifty pounds in the shop.
SILVIA   Yes, that way we'd get our money back.
PETER   And the customers would be happy.

6C Listening

Exercise 1

MR WILSON   Good morning. Sales Department.
SILVIA   Good morning, my name is Silvia Adario. I'm calling from the Perfect Partners group. Could I speak to Mr Wilson, please?
MR WILSON   Speaking. Good morning, Miss Adario. What can I do for you?

SILVIA   My colleague Teresa Volpe wrote to you recently and we received your sales material. We're interested in ordering some T-shirts to give away as Christmas gifts to our customers. We understand we can create our own design. Is that right?
MR WILSON   Yes, that's right. You send us a deposit and we produce a proof garment from your design.
SILVIA   We are a little anxious about the delivery times. You see, we need the goods by mid-November at the latest.
MR WILSON   Yes, I see. Well, if you send your order off now, you should receive our proof garment in two weeks.
SILVIA   Two weeks?
MR WILSON   Well, we could make it one week if you write a note saying it's urgent.
SILVIA   Good.
MR WILSON   Then if you send us the order, we can send you the invoice immediately.
SILVIA   By return of post?
MR WILSON   By return of post, yes. The only problem is we have to wait for your payment before we can start production.
SILVIA   If we fax you a copy of our banker's order, would you accept that or do you wait until the money is credited to your account?
MR WILSON   I'm afraid we have to wait until we receive the money. But it usually takes three or four days at the most.
SILVIA   Okay, I think I understand. Thank you, Mr Wilson. You've been most helpful.

6C Pronunciation

Exercise 1

How can I help you?
We can send the invoice immediately.

Exercise 3

A Can you confirm that we will receive the goods by Friday?
B Yes, I can. The goods will be with you on Thursday.
A And can we send them back if we don't like them?
B You certainly can. But you have to send them back the same day.

Tapescript

7A Listening

Exercise 2

SILVIA You have some wonderful things. I really like that rug on the wall. Where does it come from?

PETER That? Teresa got it in Turkey last Spring. We were on a trip buying things for the shop.

MAREK It's beautiful!

PETER It was quite funny really. When we bought it, I mean.

MAREK Why?

PETER Well, we were in the market and we saw it and both fell in love with it. So, I asked the man how much he wanted for it. He said it was seven hundred dollars. It was really nice but seven hundred was just too much so I said I couldn't take it.

TERESA Well, I couldn't believe it. I mean he didn't even try to bring the price down. I told him to try to bargain …

PETER Well, I was much too polite to bargain with him.

TERESA So I did it. Well, in L'Aquila, where I come from in Italy, we bargain all the time.

PETER It took a few minutes, but she left holding this big package.

MAREK How much did you pay for it, Teresa?

TERESA Guess!

MAREK I can't.

TERESA Go on!

MAREK Six hundred dollars?

TERESA You're joking!

MAREK Five hundred dollars?

TERESA Five hundred dollars? You can buy a car for five hundred dollars!

MAREK How much then?

TERESA Three hundred and fifty dollars. That's half what the man asked for. And he was happy, too. I expect he paid about two hundred dollars for it.

MAREK You know, Teresa, you're really good at that kind of thing. You'll have to be our Head of Purchasing.

Exercise 5

Story 1

I never bargain. I think it's wrong to ask for a special price. But I understood once that I was wrong. I was in a market in Sicily and I was buying some jeans. The man wanted forty-five thousand lire for them. That seemed like a good price to me. They were at least ninety thousand lire in the shops. So I paid forty-five thousand lire and took the jeans. But I could see the man was not happy. He was offended, like I didn't want to play his game. Or perhaps he felt that his price was too low and that he had made a mistake.

Story 2

I love bargaining. It's a real art. I remember the first time I did it was almost by mistake. I didn't want to bargain. It was in Tunisia. I saw this really beautiful headscarf and I really wanted to buy it. It was my last day on holiday and I didn't have much money left. I only had six dinar. Anyway, the man wanted ten dinar for the scarf. It was a lot of money but the scarf was really special. Anyway, I didn't have that much money, so I turned away to go. Then the man called me back. 'How much do you want to spend?' he asked. I explained that I only had six dinar and he said I could have it for that. Just over half what he asked for it. I couldn't believe it!

7B Dictation

BOSS Could you e-mail Steven Mason at Arctex for me, I don't seem to have their address.

SECRETARY Sure. Let me see. Right, that's mason s: M–A–S–O–N–S at Arctex: A–R–C–T–E–X. Do you want me to copy it to anyone?

BOSS Yes, José Perez in Sales.

SECRETARY So, cc perez j: P–E–R–E–Z–J. Right, what shall I say?

BOSS 'Steven, Your consignment of VX fittings,' comma, // 'order number // 7B414' comma, // 'was dispatched this morning. // Could you please let me know // once you have taken delivery. // Best regards, Brad Nelson.' //

SECRETARY Let me just read that back to you. So that's: 'mason s …'

7C Listening

Exercise 2

JACK Hello.

PETER Hello. Is that you, Jack?

JACK Yes, it's me. Who's calling?

PETER This is Peter.

JACK Crocodile Pete himself! How are you?

PETER Am I disturbing you? Is it a good time to call?

JACK Sure, I wasn't doing anything particular. As a matter of fact I'm on a train.

PETER So am I.

JACK Going somewhere nice?

PETER I hope so.

JACK Excuse me, that's my other mobile ringing. Hang on a minute.

PETER Your other mobile! You mean you have two?

JACK Sure! One's my private number and one's for work. Now, what can I do for you?

PETER I wanted to ask you for a telephone number.

JACK Shoot!

PETER Do you remember that man at the party last week? The one who sells special cards?

JACK Yeah. Alan Walker.

PETER That's it. Alan Walker. Do you have his number?

JACK Not on me, but I can let you have it after the weekend. I'm going on a course this weekend to improve my business skills.

PETER No! Really? So am I. At a hotel near Gatwick Airport.

JACK That's the one.

PETER Hey, we might be on the same train. What can you see out of the window?

JACK Right now I can see a field with some cows.

PETER And a red tractor?

JACK Yeah, a red tractor. We must be on the same train. See you in the coffee bar.

PETER Sure. I'll be right there!

Exercise 5

1 BILL Hello, is that Jeff? This is Bill.

JEFF Hi, Bill. We were worried. Aren't you coming to the meeting?

BILL Yes, I am. I'm just ringing to say I'll be a few minutes late.

JEFF Okay. We'll start without you then.

BILL Fine. See you later then. Bye.

2 MICK Susan, this is Mick. I can't find the right office for that small parcel, and it's raining.

SUSAN Poor Mick! Where are you now?

MICK I'm outside the main entrance of the main building.

SUSAN Right. Go round to the back of that building. There are two doors …

MICK I can't hear you properly. The line's … breaking up … Hello?

SUSAN That's better. Right, there are two doors. You want the second one. Then call them on the intercom.

MICK Great, thanks.

Exercise 1

a Is it a good time to call?

b … wasn't doing …

c I wanted to ask you …

d The one who sells special cards.

e … business skills.

f And a red tractor.

Exercise 2

a Thank goodness!

b A bunch of flowers.

c She's Susan.

d A big car.

e What do you do?

f A top business person.

8A Reading

Exercise 2

SILVIA I really like Peter, you know. He's good fun.

TERESA Good fun! You're joking. He's so bossy, always telling me what to do. I mean, he's my cousin and I like him, but I don't see him very much after work. He has his friends and I have mine.

SILVIA I see. Does he have a lot of friends?

TERESA He doesn't have a girlfriend, if that's what you mean. I think he fancies you.

SILVIA Don't be silly! Of course he doesn't.

TERESA Why not?

SILVIA Has he said anything?

Exercise 3

MAREK Is Teresa going out with Peter?

JACK No, of course not. Anyway, he's her cousin.

MAREK Yes, of course. She's so nice. Warm and friendly and funny. I really like her.

JACK Yes, she is nice, I suppose.

MAREK You're not very enthusiastic.

JACK Yes, well, she's just not my type.

MAREK Do you mean you asked her out? You asked her out and she said 'no'? Is that what happened?

JACK Yes, well, I don't think she likes English men.

8B Dictation

Can you send two similar letters to the following people, please: Mrs Jackson, that's J–A–C–K–S–O–N. // She is

Tapescript

interested in kitchen equipment. // Draw her attention to page forty-eight // and offer her a ten per cent discount. Have you got that? Mrs Jackson, // kitchen equipment, // get her to look at page forty-eight and offer a ten per cent discount. //

Then can you write one to write to Mr Beauchamp. That's B–E–A–U–C–H–A–M–P // and draw his attention to pages fifty-six and fifty-seven. // He bought a lot of garden equipment last year. // Offer him a fifteen per cent discount. // To recap, that's Mr Beauchamp, about gardening equipment. Get him to look at pages fifty-six and fifty-seven and offer a fifteen per cent discount.

8C Listening

Exercise 2

RECEPTIONIST Hello.
CALLER Hello?
RECEPTIONIST Hello. Who's speaking?
CALLER Hello. Is that Sharpe's Deliveries?
RECEPTIONIST Yes.
CALLER Can I speak to someone about a delivery please?
RECEPTIONIST Delivery? What delivery?
CALLER My name is Thomas. I need to check the delivery date for a consignment.
RECEPTIONIST Just a moment. (*music*) Hello? There's no one around at the moment. You could try calling back this afternoon. I think they're at lunch.
CALLER Can I leave a message?
RECEPTIONIST Oh dear. I'm just going off for my lunch, so it would be better if you call back. Bye.
CALLER Goodbye and thank you – for nothing .

8C Pronunciation

a I'll get him to call you back.
b I'll get back to you as soon as I can.
c Thank you for calling Perfect Partners.
d Hold the line, please. I'm putting you through.
e How can I help you?
f Have a nice day.

9A Listening

Exercise 2

AGENT Good afternoon. Can I help you?
HILTON Yes, I'd like to send a consignment of garments to Barcelona, Spain.
AGENT What's your name and address?
HILTON Waistcoats, 125 Weston Street, Boston, MA, 02113.
AGENT Who are they for?
HILTON Silvia Adario, and her phone number in Barcelona is 3485–63920.
AGENT How many boxes are there?
HILTON Three.
AGENT Have you numbered them?
HILTON Yes, W 1–3.
AGENT Are they fragile?
HILTON No.
AGENT What's in them?
HILTON Waistcoats.
AGENT What are the dimensions?
HILTON Eh, fifty-nine centimetres by forty-three by thirty-three.
AGENT And the weight?
HILTON The gross weight is thirty-nine kilograms, each box is thirteen kilograms.
AGENT And today's date is the fifteenth …

9C Listening

Exercise 1

SILVIA I'd like to speak to George Hilton, please.
SWITCHBOARD Just a moment.
HILTON Good morning. Hilton speaking.
SILVIA This is Silvia Adario from Barcelona.
HILTON Oh, hello Silvia.
SILVIA Have you heard about the accident?
HILTON Accident? Oh yes, I have. And your waistcoats were damaged. What would you like me to do?
SILVIA Have you any more available?
HILTON Well, not as many as you ordered. You asked for seventy-five and we only have fifty available today. But we could produce another twenty-five by the end of next week. Let me see, by Friday the twentieth.
SILVIA The end of next week! But I need them now.
HILTON Yes, well, I'm afraid we have a lot of orders.
SILVIA Yes, but my goods were damaged. Can't you do something about it? Can't you help me?
HILTON Yes, I appreciate how you feel. Look, I'll talk to my production manager, and I'll get back to you later in the day.
SILVIA Thank you. And can you send them by air freight?

HILTON Yes, and I'll send someone to the airport with them.

SILVIA Oh good. But I must have the waistcoats by the seventeenth.

HILTON Okay, Silvia, I'll see what I can do. And I'll be in touch later.

SILVIA Thank you. Goodbye.

9C Pronunciation

Exercise 2
A I'm afraid we only have fifty available today.
B But I asked for seventy.
A I know but they could only send us fifty. The other twenty are coming.
B But when are they coming?
A Next Monday.
B But I need them this Monday.

10A Listening

Exercise 4
SILVIA Hello, can I speak to Peter, please? This is Silvia. I'm calling from Spain.

TERESA Hi, Silvia, it's me, Teresa. How are you?

SILVIA Fine. But I need to speak to Peter urgently. Is he there?

TERESA Just a minute, I'll call him. Peter! It's Silvia for you.

PETER Oh good! … Hello?

SILVIA Hello, Peter! Listen, I've had a letter from Classic T-shirts. It's very annoying. They say Jack hasn't paid for those T-shirts yet, you know, the ones they sent in May. Listen: 'We therefore have to ask you and the other members of your group to pay us the outstanding amount as agreed, *et cetera, et cetera* …'

PETER I know, we had a letter from them this morning.

SILVIA What's the matter with your friend Jack? Why hasn't he paid yet?

PETER Look, I don't really know anything about it yet. I'll call him and find out what's going on.

SILVIA Yes, please do that! I can't afford to pay his bills.

PETER No, of course you can't. None of us can. It's really very annoying.

SILVIA It is. And I'm worried. It gives us all a bad reputation.

PETER Look, Silvia, I'm really very sorry about it. I thought Jack was reliable. Look, I'll call him straight away and find out if he's paid yet. But Silvia?

SILVIA Yes?

PETER Are you still coming to see us next month?

SILVIA Yes, of course. I've already booked my tickets. I'll be with you on the fifth.

PETER That's great. I can't wait to see you again.

SILVIA I'm looking forward to it too. But Peter …

PETER Yes?

SILVIA Sort out your friend!

PETER I will. Don't worry. Bye.

SILVIA Bye.

PETER Hey Teresa! Silvia has already had a letter from Classic T-shirts. Do you know if Marek's had one yet?

10A Speaking

Exercise 1
1 TERESA Have you paid for the new T-shirts yet?
  PETER Yes, I have. I did it this morning.

2 TERESA Have you written to the Venezuelan Embassy yet?
  PETER Oh no, I haven't. Don't worry, I'll do it soon.

3 TERESA Have you enquired about Spanish language courses?
  PETER No, not yet, but I'm going to do it this morning.

4 PETER Haven't you chosen the new supplier for toys yet?
  TERESA Oh no, I haven't. Don't worry, I'll do it now.

5 PETER Have you found a new cleaner for the shop?
  TERESA No, not yet, but I'm going to do it later this afternoon.

6 PETER Have you arranged an appointment with the Chamber of Commerce?
  TERESA Yes, I have. I did it yesterday.

10B Dictation

Dear Mr Beale, // Regarding your former property // at La Plaza San José //number twelve, // second floor, apartment B, // there is an outstanding amount // of ten thousand one hundred and fifty pesetas // dating from July // nineteen ninety-eight. // Please refer to the enclosed statement. // The new owner,' comma, // 'Mr Hedon,' that's H–E–D–O–N, comma, // 'advises us that this amount // should be paid by you. // If that is so,' comma, // 'I kindly ask you to pay this amount // to us', full stop. // 'Yours sincerely, Carlos Manuel R Moldes.'

Tapescript

10C Listening

Exercise 1

1 Julia. Hi it's Gary. You remember me? We met at Anne's party. I really enjoyed talking to you. Look I was wondering if I could see you some time this week. Would you like to go out for a meal? I'll call you later. Or you can call me on 0181–664–5829. See you!

2 Hello. This is Margaret Clinton of Malden Motors. I'm calling to enquire about your promotional T-shirts. We'd like to order two thousand if the price is right. Can you call me back on 0181–979–6442 please? Thank you.

3 Hello? Hello? Oh it's an answerphone. Is Julia Weston there? This is John Smith from Print-it-Right. A message for Julia Weston. I'm afraid I can't meet you tomorrow as arranged. Would Friday morning be possible? Can you call me back on 0171–788–8045?

4 Hello. This is Jerry Ford of Homeloans Inc. It's about your loan repayment. Your repayment was scheduled for July fifteenth. I'm afraid this payment is now overdue. Could you call me please, at your earliest convenience, to let me know what you intend to do about it? You can get me on 0171–345–6767. Thank you.

Exercise 2

Hello. This is the Premier Business School, New York. If you require information about course availability, entry qualifications and fees, please press three. For information about a specific course, please press thirty-one for marketing, thirty-two for accounting, thirty-three for benchmarking, thirty-four for contract law. If you need information about your account, please press four. For information about accommodation available in New York, please press five. If you need to speak to your tutor, please press your personal student code number. Thank you for calling. Have a nice day.

10C Speaking

Exercise 2

This is Gifts Galore, London's most original souvenir shop. I'm sorry there's no one here to take your call. Please leave your message, name and number after the bleep. We'll get back to you as soon as possible. Thank you for calling Gifts Galore.

10C Pronunciation

Exercise 1

We regret that the theatre is full today and there are no seats available. Tonight Max Graves will play the part of Hamlet.

Exercise 2

a You have to heat the water before you make tea.
b Have you finished your chat?
c Luke is a very lucky businessman.
d The exam was hard.
e Our company bid for the contract.
f We have to pull together in the company.

11A Listening

Exercise 2

1 Well, people say I'm very outgoing and that I have a good sense of humour but I think I'm more serious than that. I would say I was hard-working and quite confident.

2 Oh yes, I think I am. I'm very tidy and like to keep everything in the right place. I'm methodical, too. You know, I write myself lists so I don't forget to do things. And I think I can supervise other people's work too, if that's what you mean.

3 For four years. I came here after I left college. I really like it here. I don't really want to go back home.

4 Well, it's a good job, but it's a really big company and you feel a bit anonymous sometimes, like you're not important and the work's the same every day. I'd like a bit more variety.

11C Listening

Exercise 2

MAREK Good morning Anna. How are you?
ANNA Fine thanks Marek, and you?
MAREK Fine thanks.
ANNA What do you want me to do this morning?
MAREK I've got a few calls for you to make first. Have you got a pen and paper? Good. You can write these down. I've changed my plans for next week. I'm going to stay in Manchester until Friday morning. So could you call Mr Hix in Birmingham, 0121–389–67589. He's one of the trade fair people. Apologize and say I'll be busy on Thursday. Ask him if Monday would be convenient.

ANNA   Okay, will do.

MAREK   Then I have to cancel lunch with Mr Gaston on Thursday. He's the manager of the toy shop. His number is 543–5670. See if he can see me on Tuesday.

ANNA   Is that lunch on Tuesday?

MAREK   If he can make it, lunch would be fine.

ANNA   Right.

MAREK   Then, could you set up a meeting with that woman I met last week. Remember? Her name's Roberta Miller. I really think she will be a good contact to have.

ANNA   Do you have her number, Marek?

MAREK   It's 857–3902. Find out when she's available and tell her I'll call to confirm.

ANNA   Fine.

MAREK   Oh, and Anna, cancel all my appointments on Friday, will you? I'm going up to Scotland with Teresa for the weekend. And thinking of Teresa, call her too, and ask her if she can come to Manchester on Wednesday to help me with the presentation. Tell her I'll pay for her flight and she can be back in London by five o'clock.

11C   Pronunciation

Exercise 1

a thirteenth   **c** fifteen   **e** eighty
b seventy   **d** twentieth

12A   Reading

Exercise 3

CUSTOMER   Excuse me. I bought this mug in your shop last week and …

PETER   Do you have a receipt?

CUSTOMER   Yes, here it is. I bought this mug in your shop last week and it's cracked.

PETER   Yes, I can see it's cracked. Did you drop it?

CUSTOMER   No, it was cracked when I took it out of the bag.

PETER   But sir, we inspect all mugs before we wrap them. We always notice if there's a crack. Look, you bought it a week ago. How can you be sure you didn't damage it?

CUSTOMER   Because I put it away as soon as I got home. Why don't you listen to me?

PETER   I'm afraid we don't give refunds. Look at the notice on that wall: 'Please inspect goods at the moment of sale as we cannot give refunds.'

CUSTOMER   Well, that's ridiculous. I've never heard such nonsense. I'm never buying anything here again!

Exercise 5

CUSTOMER   Excuse me. I bought this mug in your shop last week and it's cracked.

TERESA   I see. Do you have the receipt please? … Thank you.

CUSTOMER   I didn't drop it or anything, I put it carefully away because it was a birthday present for my mother. When I got it out, this morning, to give to her I saw that it was cracked.

TERESA   I am sorry sir. We usually inspect all mugs before we wrap them. Perhaps we didn't check this one properly.

CUSTOMER   Well, can you give me a refund?

TERESA   I'm afraid it's not our policy to give refunds. But would you like to exchange it for another mug?

CUSTOMER   That would be fine. Thank you.

12A   Listening

Exercise 1

TERESA   What are these?

PETER   Oh they're great, aren't they?

TERESA   Oh Peter, do me a favour! They're so badly made. One of them is broken already! No wonder customers are complaining!

PETER   Well, I can't send them back now! I've already paid for them.

TERESA   Give them to your friend Jack! He'd like them. Oh Peter, we promised we would only sell original, good quality products.

PETER   You're so serious, Teresa.

TERESA   Well you can't just make decisions without asking my opinion.

PETER   But you just say 'no'. You know Teresa, we're not really enjoying this any more are we?

TERESA   I don't like serving in the shop.

PETER   And I don't like living in London.

TERESA   Well, we could always sell. I could go in with Marek. But what would you do? Go back to Australia?

PETER   Well, actually, no. The truth is it's Silvia. I just want to be with her all the time.

TERESA   But, Peter, that's great. How about Silvia? Does she feel the same way?

PETER   I guess she does. I'm sorry, Teresa, my heart's not in this any more. I don't want to be here, I want to be in Barcelona.

Tapescript

12B Dictation

Dear Mr Newton, // Thank you for informing us // about the damage done // to some of the shoes we sent you // on the nineteenth of July // (order number 3973). // We appreciate the problems this has caused you // and hope we can find a solution // by the end of this week. // Could you please keep // the whole consignment // in your warehouse // so that we can inspect the damage // for insurance purposes? // We will send replacements // a.s.a.p. // Unfortunately, // we do not have everything you need in stock. //
Yours sincerely, …

12C Listening

Exercise 1

1 PETER Hello. This is Peter Clapton.
JEWELLER Hello sir. How can I help you?
PETER I'm calling about the ring I bought last week. It was a diamond and sapphire engagement ring. Can you tell me if it's ready yet?
JEWELLER I'm sorry, I didn't catch your name.
PETER Clapton, C–L–A–P–T–O–N.
JEWELLER I'm sorry, sir, it hasn't come back from cleaning yet. I'll call you as soon as it's in.
PETER I'm afraid it's quite urgent. I'm planning to go to Barcelona on the fifth and I must have it before then.
JEWELLER Very well, sir, I understand. I'll make sure it's here tomorrow afternoon.

2 TRAVEL AGENT Hello. Could I help you?
PETER Yes, can you check if there are any seats available for a flight to Barcelona please?
TRAVEL AGENT Yes, sir. When are you thinking of flying?
PETER On the morning of the fifth. The first available flight.
TRAVEL AGENT Is six twenty too early?
PETER No, that's fine. Well, maybe it is a little early. Have you got something a bit later?
TRAVEL AGENT There's a flight at eleven that gets in at two thirty.
PETER That would be great. How much is it?
TRAVEL AGENT Two hundred and nine pounds.
PETER Fine.
TRAVEL AGENT What's the name please sir?
PETER Clapton. Mr Peter Clapton.
TRAVEL AGENT How would you like to pay, sir?

PETER I'll pay on my credit card.
TRAVEL AGENT Could you give me the card number and expiry date please sir?
PETER Sure, it's 5226 …

3 PETER Hello Manuel, it's Peter from England.
MANUEL Hello Peter, I'll call Silvia.
PETER No, no. I don't want to speak to her. I want to speak to you. Listen, I'm coming to Barcelona on Sunday.
MANUEL Sunday.
PETER That's right, on Sunday afternoon. But you mustn't tell Silvia. I want it to be a surprise.
MANUEL A surprise. Why?
PETER I want you do something for me. Can you keep a secret?
MANUEL Of course I can keep a secret. But what are you going to do?
PETER I'm going to take Silvia out to dinner. Can you book me a table at a good restaurant?
MANUEL Do you know El Limonero?
PETER Yes, that would be perfect. For nine o'clock. Table for two, Manuel.
MANUEL Yes, yes. I don't want to come!
PETER Then can you bring her along? Think of some reason. But don't let her know it's me. And Manuel …
MANUEL Yes.
PETER Can you arrange for candles and flowers, something really romantic, roses perhaps …

4 RECEPTIONIST Correda Hotel.
PETER Hello I'd like to book a room for a week, please, from Sunday the fifth.
RECEPTIONIST Sunday the fifth. Yes, sir, is that a single room or a double?
PETER A single room, please, with a bathroom.
RECEPTIONIST Of course, sir. All our rooms have bathrooms.
PETER Can you give me a price for that?
RECEPTIONIST Yes, that's eleven thousand five hundred pesetas.
PETER Right. That's fine.
RECEPTIONIST Can you confirm the booking in writing, please.
PETER Yes, sure. I'll fax it through immediately. Can you give me your fax number?
RECEPTIONIST Sure it's 91742 …

12C Pronunciation

Exercise 1

a I asked her to cash it.
b Three new products for you to try.
c How many shares do you have?
d There's a fire in the shop.
e My mouse isn't working!

12C Speaking

Exercise 5

MAREK I'm really pleased for you, Peter. I'm sure you and Silvia will be really happy.

PETER Thank you, Marek. I think we will. But what about you? Are you going to stay single all your life? I thought you and Teresa …

MAREK Oh, no! We're just friends. Anyway, I think Teresa wants to go back to Italy.

PETER Really? I thought she was happy in London.

MAREK Well, you know, she's been doing some presentations for me up in Manchester and Glasgow?

PETER Yes, she told me about that.

MAREK Well, she's really good at it. She can really sell ideas. You know, get ideas across.

PETER Well, good old Teresa!

MAREK And now she's thinking of doing it as a career. She speaks excellent English, she's got a lot of experience in business now you know, with the shop and the agency. I think she could get a really good job.

PETER Yes, I see what you mean. And just think, only three years ago Teresa and I didn't know what we wanted to do. Then we got the shop, met you and Silvia, started our group … We've come a long way!!

13A Listening

Exercise 2

PETER … That's really interesting.

MR TAYLOR Yes, there are a lot of good things about being a franchisee.

PETER Just a minute, Mr Taylor. Franchisee – is that the person who buys into the franchise or the one who sells it?

MR TAYLOR The one who buys in. The one who sells the franchise is called the franchisor.

PETER Okay. I think I've got it now.

MR TAYLOR You benefit from the franchisor's good reputation and sales record, but of course, it's not cheap. A large part of your sales income normally goes to the franchisor.

PETER Right, but what about control over the business?

MR TAYLOR Well, you don't, and never will have, complete control.

PETER Just a minute, I thought you said there were a lot of good things about being a franchisor … I mean a franchisee.

MR TAYLOR Well, there are. I've already mentioned the franchisor's image and track record in sales. Plus you get a lot of help, for example, with your administration and with … training. And of course with marketing. And if the franchisor is doing well, then you'll do well too.

PETER But then if, for some reason, the franchisor gets into difficulties, you lose your good reputation, too.

MR TAYLOR Yes, certainly. You have to be careful when you choose which company to buy into. Very careful.

Exercise 5

PETER I've been looking at franchising.

SILVIA Franchising?

PETER Why not? We've got enough money to buy into a franchise.

SILVIA Yes, but why?

PETER Well, I think everything would be easier. There would be less work.

SILVIA Do you think so?

PETER Yes, because the franchisor would tell us what to do.

SILVIA But don't you like being your own boss?

PETER Well, I do, yes. But with franchising we'd have the best of both worlds.

SILVIA I don't understand.

PETER I mean, we'd still be the boss but we'd have fewer responsibilities; and there'd be fewer decisions to take.

SILVIA Yes, that's true. You mean, we'd have more time for ourselves.

Grammar reference

Adverbs of frequency

never	sometimes	often	usually	always
0%		50%		100%

Adverbs of frequency come after the verb *be* and before other verbs:

*Teresa is **never** late for an appointment.*
*Teresa **never** listens to Peter.*

Put the adverbs in brackets in the correct position.

EXAMPLE
We give discounts. (never)
We never give discounts.

a I go to work by train. (always)
b He is very patient. (usually)
c They were on time. (never)
d She forgets to ring people back. (sometimes)
e I am out of the office on Fridays. (often)

Articles

a / an is used with a singular countable noun which we talk about for the first time:
*A man came in this morning to buy **a** present.*

After that, we refer to the same person or thing with *the*:
***The** man asked me to wrap **the** present.*

Before a consonant sound we use *a*. Before a vowel sound we use *an*:
*a present, a chair, **an** exam, **an** old man*

But we say: ***an** hour, **a** unit.*

The article we use depends on the sound, not the spelling.

the is used when we talk about a particular thing:
***The** film I saw last night was very good.*
***The** station is near **the** town centre.*

the is usually used before:	*the* is not usually used before:
whole family names: *the Smiths*	people's names: *Mr Smith, Paul Smith*
plural place names: *the United States*	the names of countries: *England, Spain*
names of rivers, seas: *the Thames* *the Mediterranean*	names of cities, towns, lakes, and mountains: *Rome, Mount Everest*

Complete the gaps with *a*, *an*, *the*, or no article (ø).

Last year I went to __ø__ France. I stayed in __1____ hotel in __2____ Paris. __3____ hotel was near __4____ River Seine. At __5____ hotel, I met __6____ man called __7____ Jean Gaudin. He invited me to his family house. It was __8____ old house in __9____ middle of __10____ big forest.

Comparatives and superlatives

Example	Comparative	Superlative
one syllable:		
cheap	cheaper	the cheapest
big	bigger	the biggest
two or more syllables:		
advanced	more advanced	the most advanced
profitable	less profitable	the least profitable
adjectives ending in -*y*:		
easy	easier	the easiest
busy	busier	the busiest
irregular adjectives:		
good	better	the best
bad	worse	the worst
far	farther / further	the farthest / furthest

– Some two-syllable adjectives take -*er* and -*est*:
*The new machine is **quieter**.*
*That's the **simplest** answer.*
If you are unsure of a particular word, check in a good dictionary.

– *than* is used after a comparative to say that two things are different:
*Plastic is cheaper **than** leather.*
*This product is less profitable **than** that one.*

– The superlative is used for three or more things:
*This is **the most interesting** offer I have had.*

– *as … as* is used to say things are similar:
*Shoes are **as profitable as** clothes.*

1 What are the comparative and superlative forms of these adjectives?

EXAMPLE
satisfying   *more satisfying*   *most satisfying*

a quick   c lucky   e beautiful
b difficult   d fat   f bad

2 Complete the gaps in these sentences with one word.

EXAMPLE
My car is more expensive *than* your car.

a It was ——— most expensive present in the shop.
b It was more expensive ——— a diamond ring.
c Russian is ——— difficult than English.
d This exercise is not ——— easy as the last one.
e This is the ——— interesting book I've read.

Conditionals

We use conditional sentences to talk about how likely an event is to happen.

Possible situations
To describe a present situation (the *if*-clause) with a possible future result (the main clause), use:

if + present simple + *will* + infinitive without *to*
If Teresa **has** time, she**'ll write** to the supplier today.

Improbable situations
To describe something which is very unlikely to happen, use:

if + past simple + *would* + infinitive without *to*
If Peter **won** a lot of money, he **would buy** a bigger shop. (but he probably won't)

– The *if*-clause can also come at the end of the sentence:
She**'ll miss** the train **if** she's late.

– *Unless* is often used, meaning *if not*:
Unless you pay, my lawyer will contact you.

1 Complete these sentences with the correct form of the verbs in brackets.

a If I see him, I (tell) him you want to speak to him.
b If they like them, they (buy) a lot.
c If she (be) rich, she would travel around the world.
d What will you do if you (not make) a profit?
e They (order) more, if he had more to sell.

2 Think of four ways to complete each of these two sentences.

a If I won a lot of money, I …
b If the weather is good tomorrow, I …

Conjunctions

Conjuctions join two clauses to form one sentence.
– *and, but, and, or* join two main clauses:
I went to France **and** (I went to) Germany.
I went to Paris, **but** I didn't see the Eiffel Tower.
Next year I'd like to go to Italy **or** (I'd like to go to) Spain.

– *when, if, because, as* join a sub-clause to the main clause. The sub-clause can go before or after the main clause:
When it arrives, I'll call you.
I'll call you **when** it arrives.

If I ask him, he'll come.
He'll come **if** I ask him.

As / Because I think you'll like it, I'll give it to you.
I'll give it to you **as / because** I think you'll like it.

– *which* and *who* are also conjunctions: see **Relative clauses**, page 121.

Join these sentences using the word in brackets.

EXAMPLE
I work very hard. I'm not very rich. (but)
I work very hard, but I'm not very rich.

a I like swimming. / I don't like running. (but)
b I bought a new computer. It helps me to do my job. (which)
c I get paid. / I'll buy some new CDs. (when)
d You can pick it up. You can have it delivered. (or)

Countable and uncountable nouns

Countable nouns have plural forms:
chair / chairs, man / men

– The verb must agree with the number:
*Three people **are** here to see you.*
*The chair **is** broken.*

– To ask questions about countable nouns we use *how many*:
How many books do you need?
How many people work here?

– Use *many* and *any* for the negative form:
He **hasn't** got **many** friends.
We **haven't** got **any** books.

Uncountable nouns do not have plural forms:
money, water, information

Grammar reference

- They often refer to abstract ideas like *love* and *freedom*, or to activities like *work* and *travel*.

- Some uncountable nouns like *news* and *mathematics* end in *-s*, but they are singular, not plural.

- Uncountable nouns always have a singular verb:
  *This information **is** very useful.*
  *Commerce **is** fascinating.*

- Some uncountable nouns in English are countable in other languages, so be careful!

  These words are never countable:

accommodation	news
advice	permission
furniture	progress
homework	traffic
information	weather
money	work

  *His work **is** very good.*
  *How much money **is** there in the account?*
  *I need **some** advice about my account.*

- To ask questions about them we use *how much*:
  ***How much** money do you earn?*
  ***How much** information do you need?*

- Use *much* and *any* for the negative form:
  *I **don't** have **much** information about that company.*
  *They **don't** do **any** work.*

- Some nouns can be countable and uncountable, depending on their meaning:
  Two coffees, please. (this tells us the quantity)
  I like coffee. (this tells us a general fact)

1 Are the following words countable or uncountable?

a table   d water   g book
b woman   e business   h money
c information   f milk   i job

2 Match these countable and uncountable nouns.

EXAMPLE
suggestion: advice

a knowledge   e suitcase
b luggage   f job
c work   g house
d accommodation   h fact

Future

We use different forms to talk about the future.

be going to
To describe intentions, use:
be + going to + infinitive without to
*I**'m going to stay** in England for a month.* (I haven't bought my ticket yet.)

present continuous
To describe something that is a definite arrangement, use:
be + present participle
*I**'m arriving** at ten o'clock.* (I've got my ticket.)
*How long **are** you **staying**?*
*He**'s not coming** until tomorrow.*

future simple
When we are sure about the future, we use:
will + infinitive without to

- statements of fact:
  *He**'ll be** away all day.* (It's in his diary.)
  *How long **will** it **take**?*
  *We **won't be** here tomorrow.*

- promising, or deciding at the time of speaking, to do something:
  *I**'ll fax** the order right away.*
  ***Will** you **do** me a favour?*

present simple
This is used for timetables and schedules. It doesn't depend on how sure we are.
*The plane **leaves** at ten o'clock.*
*What time **does** it **arrive** in London?*
*The film **doesn't start** until eight o'clock.*

1 Choose the correct future form in brackets.

SALESMAN I haven't got the time to pick up my traveller's cheques today.
ADMINISTRATOR Don't worry, (I'll get / I'm getting) them for you.
SALESMAN What time (is my flight / is my flight going to be)?
ADMINISTRATOR It (leaves / will leave) at three o'clock. (Do you drive / Are you driving) to the airport?
SALESMAN No, I (get / am going to get) a taxi.
ADMINISTRATOR Fine, (I'll phone / I'm phoning) to book one for you.
SALESMAN Thanks.

2 Which of these sentences:
- – is a promise?
- – expresses an intention?
- – is a plan / arrangement?
- – is a fact about the future?
- – relates to a schedule / timetable?

a When are you visiting the trade fair?
b Don't worry. I won't tell anybody.
c What time do the banks close?
d They are going to look for some new suppliers.
e He'll be free at seven o' clock.

Future time clauses

Future time clauses with *when*, *after*, and *before* are used when we are sure an event will happen;
I **will decide** what to do **after** I speak to him.
When I know the flight times, I **will book** a ticket.

- The form is the same as future conditional clauses with *if* (see **Conditionals**, page 113).
- The verb in the time clause is in the present simple, the verb in the main clause is in the future.

Complete these sentences with the present simple or the future simple form of the verbs in brackets.

a We will send a letter of acknowledgement when we (receive) your order.
b After they receive your deposit, they (print) the brochures.
c They will do nothing before the bank (notify) them about payment.

make and *do*

It can be difficult to decide when to use *make* and *do*. Here are some common expressions:

You *make*	You *do*
an arrangement	business
a call	the cleaning
a decision	a course in
an enquiry	a deal
an offer	someone a favour
money	a job
a promise	research
progress	the shopping
a suggestion	some work
a complaint	your best
a mistake	good

Complete these sentences with an appropriate form of *make* or *do*.

a I must go and _____ some work now.
b I'm _____ a course in time management.
c The food was terrible, so I _____ a complaint.
d We're _____ progress.
e She _____ an offer I couldn't refuse.

Measurements

To measure	Metric units	Abbreviation
distance, height, size	millimetre	mm
	centimetre	cm
	metre	m
	kilometre	km
weight	milligram	mg
	gram	g
	kilo(gram)	kg
	tonne	t
volume	millilitre	ml
	centilitre	cl
	litre	l

Adjectives for measurements	Nouns for measurements
deep	*depth*
high (for buildings / structures)	*height*
long	*length*
tall (for people)	*height*
thick	*thickness*
wide / across	*width*

Talking about measurements
*How **high** is it?*
*It's five metres **high**.*

*How **heavy** is it?*
*It **weighs** fifteen kilograms.*

What are the dimensions? / What size is it?
*It's ten centimetres wide, **by** twenty centimetres deep, **by** four centimetres high. (10 cm x 20 cm x 4 cm)*

Ask these questions. Begin with *How …*

EXAMPLE
Ask how big the box is. *How big is the box?*
a Ask about the weight.
b Ask about the width.
c Ask about the height.

Grammar reference

Modals

Modal auxiliary verbs are used to talk about levels of certainty and obligation. They are formed in the same way as the auxiliary verbs *be* and *have*:

can / could / may / might / must / shall / should / would + infinitive without *to*

Ability *(can, can't)*:
*I **can** read Polish.   **I can't** type.*

Advice *(should)*:
*You **should** come to the meeting.*
*You **shouldn't** smoke.*

Certainty *(must, can't)*:
*There **must** be a mistake.*
*This **can't** be right.*

Obligation *(must)*:
*You **must** send this now.*
*You **musn't** order any more.*

Note: *have to* also expresses obligation, but *not have to* is used to say something is not necessary:
*I **have to** send this letter, but I **don't have to** send it today.*

Offers *(shall, can, would)*:
***Shall** I help you?*
***Can** I help you?*
***Would** you like me to help you?*

Requests *(can, would, could)*:
***Can** you help me?*
***Could** you put me through?* (more formal)
***Would** you kindly send us a catalogue?*

Suggestions *(could, couldn't, shall, would)*:
*You **could** ask Teresa.*
***Couldn't** we ask to pay later?*
***Shall** we buy more T-shirts?*

Possibility and probability *(may, could, might)*:
*You **may** get more orders.*
*It **could** be a mistake.*

1 Which of the following sentences expresses:
   – possibility / probability?
   – certainty?

   a It must be true. Three people have told me.
   b I might leave early tomorrow. It depends on how long this job will take.
   c He can't be in Spain because I saw him five minutes ago.
   d There may be some mistakes in the letter. Please tell me if you find any.

2 Choose the correct alternative in brackets in the sentences below.

   a Peter isn't sure what time his plane arrives, so he (must / might) not get here on time.
   b I sent the letter today, so he (may / can't) receive it tomorrow or the next day.
   c No, this is Teresa speaking. You (may not / must) have the wrong number.
   d It (may / can't) be her – she is in Germany at the moment.

3 Which modal verb in the following sentences expresses:

   – strong obligation?
   – advice?
   – ability?
   – an offer?
   – a request?

   a Shall I send you a better copy?
   b Could you fax confirmation, please?
   c You must deliver them this afternoon.
   d You should rewrite that.
   e Can Peter speak Spanish?

Money

Country	Currency	Symbol
Australia	dollar(s)	A$
Czech Republic	koruna / crown	Kč
France	franc(s)	F
Germany	mark(s)	DM
Great Britain	pound(s)	£
Hungary	forint(s)	Ft
Italy	lira(s / lire)	Lit
Japan	yen	¥
Poland	złoty(s)	zł
Portugal	escudo(s)	Esc
Spain	peseta(s)	Ptas
Turkey	lira(s)	TL
United States	dollar(s)	$
European Union	euros	€

To ask about the exchange rate:
How many Czech koruna are there to the German mark?
How many francs are there to the US dollar?

When there is a smaller unit (e.g. 1 Australian dollar = 100 cents) we say the amounts like this:
5F50 = five francs fifty   *£10.50 = ten pounds fifty*

Ask about these exchange rates:

EXAMPLE   Japan / Britain
How many yen are there to the pound?

a   Italy / Germany
b   Poland / France
c   Hungary / Spain

Numbers

Cardinal		Ordinal	
1	one	1st	first
2	two	2nd	second
3	three	3rd	third
4	four	4th	fourth
5	five	5th	fifth
6	six	6th	sixth
7	seven	7th	seventh
8	eight	8th	eighth
9	nine	9th	ninth
10	ten	10th	tenth
11	eleven	11th	eleventh
12	twelve	12th	twelfth
13	thirteen	13th	thirteenth
20	twenty	20th	twentieth
21	twenty-one	21st	twenty-first
22	twenty-two	22nd	twenty-second
30	thirty	30th	thirtieth
40	forty	40th	fortieth
50	fifty	50th	fiftieth
100	a / one hundred	100th	(one) hundredth
1,000	a / one thousand	1000th	(one) thousandth

Fractions
¼ *a quarter*   ½ *a half*   ⅓ *a third*

Order of adjectives

The normal order for adjectives before a noun is:

1 size   **2** colour   **3** material

If there is a number, it comes first:
Two small brown cardboard boxes.

Put the adjectives below in the correct order.

a   black twelve wooden chairs
b   one small plastic red box
c   large ten metal grey containers
d   three brown enormous cases leather
e   eight glass green bottles

Passives

When we know who or what has done something we use the active:
*The factory **produces** computers.*

The passive is used when we don't know, or it is unimportant, who / what has performed an action:

be + past participle (+ *by* + noun)
*Computers **are produced** (**by** the factory).*

–to describe processes:
*The documents **are checked**.*

–when we don't know or don't want to say who has done something:
*My salary **is paid** into my account.*

–to say who or what has done something, use *by*:
*It **is made by** hand.*

See page 122 for a list of irregular past participles.

Rewrite these sentences in the passive.

EXAMPLE
The company employs four hundred and fifty people.
Four hundred and fifty people are employed.

a   They provide free lunches for all the staff.
     Free lunches …
b   Someone cleans the office regularly.
     The office …
c   The company exports many products.
     Many products …
d   People spend a lot of money on clothing.
     A lot of money …
e   They give discounts to regular customers.
     Discounts …

Grammar reference

Past simple

be is not formed in the same way as other verbs:
I / he / she / it **was.**
I / he / she / it **was not / wasn't.**
Was *I / he / she / it?*

You / we / they **were.**
You / we / they **were not / weren't.**
Were *you / we / they?*

have is formed like this:
I / you / he / she / it / we / they **had** …
I / you / he / she / it / we / they **did not have** …
Did *I / you / he / she / it / we / they* **have** …?

– The past simple of *have got* is *had*.

– Use *did* to make questions and negative sentences with both regular and irregular verbs, in short answers, and for emphasis.

Regular verbs are formed like this:
I / you / he / she / it / we / they (+ verb + *-ed*).
I / you / he / she / it / we / they did not / didn't (+ verb).
Did I / you / he / she / it / we / they (+ verb)?
Yes, I did. / No he didn't.

– For verbs ending in *-e*, add *-d* :
He **used** the photocopier.

– For verbs ending in a consonant + *-y*, change *-y* to *-i* and add *-ed*:
He **tried** to do it.

– For verbs ending in a single vowel + consonant, double the consonant and add *-ed*:
She **travelled*** for a long time.
(* In American English: *traveled*)

See page 122 for a list of irregular verbs.

– Use the past simple to talk about finished actions in the past:
I **saw** an advertisement in yesterday's paper.
When **did** you **start** the business?

1 Complete the sentences below with the past simple of one of these verbs:

have   read   buy   travel   give   be

a She _____ us all the information we asked for.
b I _____ a very good time at the trade fair.
c I _____ very nervous before my exam yesterday.
d He _____ to Paris by train.
e I _____ about it in the newspaper.
f A woman came into the shop and _____ five hats.

2 Teresa went on a business trip. Write some questions using the following prompts:

EXAMPLE
where she went
Where did you go?

a where the hotel was
b how long she stayed there
c if the food was good
d if she went by plane

Prepositions of movement and place

I drove **to** *the shops.*	x → y
I went **by** *bus.*	x → → y
She is **at** *home.*	
My briefcase is **in** *the car.*	
He is sitting **on** *the chair.*	

Complete these sentences with appropriate prepositions.

EXAMPLE
The report is *on* your desk.

a Is she _____ the trade fair?
b Are you coming _____ the meeting?
c The new clocks are _____ the bottom cupboard.
d They arrived _____ rail.
e It's _____ the bottom of the page.

Present continuous

be + verb + *-ing*

He's (he **is**) **working.**
He's not **working.**
Is he **working**? Yes, he **is.**

Use the present continuous to talk about:

– plans and arrangements for the future:
I'm **arriving** tomorrow.
I'm not **coming** next week.   When **are** you **leaving**?

– present moment:
I'm putting you through.
I am writing to ask for some information.
He's not speaking to anyone at the moment.
Who's calling please?

– temporary situations:
We're preparing a new collection.
I'm not making much money.

1 When do the verbs in the following sentences refer to:

– the future?
– the present moment?
– a temporary situation?

a Who's calling, please?
b What are you doing after the meeting?
c We're experimenting with plastic furniture this year.
d I'm phoning about our recent order.
e I'm meeting him next week.
f What project are you working on?

2 Put the verb in the correct form, present continuous or present simple.

EXAMPLE
Who you usually (buy) from?
Who do you usually buy from?

a Teresa (come) to the next meeting.
b you (come) to the next meeting?
c I (write) to ask for a bigger discount.
d I (not work) tomorrow.
e He (speak) five languages.

Present perfect

have + past participle

I / you / we / they **have worked.**
I / you / we / they **haven't / have not worked.**
Have *I / you / we / they* **worked?**

He / she / it **has worked.**
He / she / it **hasn't / has not worked.**
Has *he / she / it* **worked?**

With regular verbs, add *-ed* to the infinitive (without *to*) to make the past participle.

See page 122 for a list of irregular past participles.

Uses of the present perfect

– situations that began in the past and which are still continuing:
How long **have** *you* **lived** *here?*
I've worked here for ten years.
He hasn't been at work for two weeks.

– past actions with present results:
He **has opened** *a new shop in New York.*
(Now he has a shop.)
I **have** *already* **posted** *the letter.*
(It is in the post.)

– experiences:
Have *you ever* **been** *to China?*
I've never used e-mail.

– We use *for* with a period of time:
for *two weeks,* **for** *five months,* **for** *a long time*

– We use *since* for a point in time:
since *last week,* **since** *October,* **since** *yesterday,*
since *1990*

1 Choose the correct alternative in brackets.

a (Have you been / Did you go) to the meeting yesterday?
b I'm looking for their order. (Have you seen it? / Did you see it?)
c Where (have you been / were you) born?
d (I've already seen it / I already saw it.) It's great.
e I (have been / went) to the trade fair with Teresa last year.

2 Complete these time expressions with *for* or *since* .

a _____ ten weeks
b _____ Tuesday
c _____ nine o'clock this morning
d _____ an hour or so

Present simple

be and *have* are not formed the same as other verbs:

be

I am	*I'm (I am) not*
Are you?	*Yes, I am.*
He / she / it is.	*He / she / it isn't.*
You / we / they are.	*You / we / they're*
Are they ?	*Yes, they are.*

Grammar reference

have

I **have**	*I* **don't (do not) have**
Do *you* **have?**	*Yes, I* **do.**
she **has**	*she* **doesn't have**
Does *she* **have…?**	*Yes, she* **does.**

– When we talk about possession, we often use *have got* not *have*:
  I **have got** */ she* **has got** *a lot of money.*
  Have *you* **got** */ has he* **got** *a lot of money? Yes, I* **have** */ he* **has.**
  (not usual in American English)

Other verbs

I / you / we / they **work.**
I / you / we / they don't **work.**
Do I / you / we / they **work?**

He / she / it **works.**
He / she / it doesn't **work.**
Does he / she / it **work?**

– Use *do* (with *I / you / we / they*) and *does* (with *he / she / it*) to make questions and negative sentences, in short answers, and for emphasis.

– With *he / she / it* add *-s* (e.g. *works, starts*) or *-es* (e.g. *pushes, goes, catches, passes, fixes, tries*).

Uses of the present simple
– general facts and information:
  They **make** *furniture.*
  They **don't make** *furniture.*
  Do *they* **make** *furniture? Yes they* **do.**

– habitual actions:
  I often **go** *to the cinema.*
  I **don't** *often* **go** *to the cinema.*
  Do *you* **go** *to the cinema often? No, I* **don't.**
  How often **do** *you* **go** *to the cinema?*

– opinions and feelings:
  He **loves** *Silvia.*
  He **doesn't love** *Silvia.*
  Does *he* **love** *Silvia? Yes, he* **does.**

1 Complete the passage with one of the verbs below in the correct form.

try	be	be	think
agree	believe	like	worry

Teresa ¹_____ quality products, so she always ²_____ to find good suppliers. She doesn't ³_____ about the price of things – quality ⁴_____ more important to

her. Does Peter ⁵_____ with her? No, he ⁶_____ that it ⁷_____ more important to get a good price, but they both ⁸_____ that the products should be unique.

2 Which of these sentences refer to:
– habitual actions?
– facts / information?
– opinions / feelings?

a The shop is in Highbury.
b I often watch television after dinner.
c What does he think of her?
d Do you usually work at weekends?
e How much does it cost?
f I love it.

Questions

Yes / No questions
When the answer to the question is *yes* or *no*, start the questions with an auxiliary or modal verb:
Are *you a shop assistant?*
Do *you like football?*
Shall *we buy more stock?*
Will *you have enough money to start a business?*

Open questions
When the answer is a full sentence, use a *wh-* question:

how (many / much) / what /
when / where / who / why + (auxiliary) verb

– Use *who* to ask about people:
  Who lives here? **Jenny** *lives here.* (asks about the subject)
  Who does Peter love? Peter loves **Silvia.** (asks about the object – *whom* is sometimes used in formal letters)
  Who is he? He's a famous film star.

– Use *what* to ask about an action or thing:
  What sells well? **T-shirts** *sell well.* (asks about the subject)
  What do you like? I like **playing tennis.** (asks about the object)
  What is his name? His name is **John.**

– Use *where* to ask about a place / location:
  Where does he live? He lives **in Hungary.**
  Where is my bag? It's **on the chair.**

– Use *when* to ask about a time:
  When did you see the film? I saw it **yesterday.**
  When is the next meeting? It's **next Tuesday.**

– Use *why* to ask for a reason:
*Why is he here? Because **he works here**.*
*Why do they make so much money? Because **they work very hard**.*

– Use *how much* to ask about quantity:
*How much did you pay? I paid **four dollars**.*

– Use *how many* to ask about a number:
*How many people work here? About **three hundred**.*

Complete these questions about the night club which Teresa goes to.

EXAMPLE
What is the club called? (name of the club)

a _____ do you go with? (the people she goes with)
b _____ do you like going there? (reason)
c _____ is the club? (location)
d _____ does it close? (closing time)
e _____ does the ticket cost? (price)
f _____ people go there? (number of people)

Relative clauses with *who* and *which*

Relative clauses can be added to a sentence to give more information about people or things.

– If the clause refers to things, it begins with *which* or *that*:
*Our latest designs, **which are all in plastic**, have won many awards.*

– If it refers to people, it begins with *who* or *that*:
*Helen, **who's in computers**, has made a fortune.*

– Note: the use of commas shows that these relative clauses add extra information. The sentences are complete without the relative clauses.
Our latest designs have won many awards.

Complete these sentences with *who* or *what*.

a The bank manager, _____ is a friend of mine, is also a good golf player.
b Our new equipment, _____ we bought from Poland, is the best of its kind.
c Let me introduce you to John, _____ wants to join our partnership.
d This is the new machine, _____ I told you about last week.

Time

Time	British English	American English
10.00	*ten* or *ten o'clock*	*ten* or *ten o'clock*
10.20	*ten twenty* *twenty past ten*	*ten twenty* *twenty after ten*
10.15	*ten fifteen* *(a) quarter past ten*	*ten fifteen* *quarter after ten*
10.30	*ten thirty* *half past ten* *half ten*	*ten thirty* *half past ten*
10.45	*ten forty-five* *(a) quarter to eleven*	*ten forty-five* *quarter of eleven*

– English generally uses the 12-hour clock (except in timetables). If the time of day is not clear from the context in spoken English, say:
in the afternoon
in the evening
in the early morning
at night

If it is not clear in written English, write:
a.m. (morning)
p.m. (afternoon or evening)

– Expressions of time with prepositions:
at ten
on Tuesday, on June the first
in May, in spring, in 1999
after ten
until / till midnight
since five this morning, for weeks
at the end of the month

Complete the time expressions in the following sentences with these prepositions:

at   on   in

a I'll see you _____ half past ten.
b The next meeting is _____ February.
c We open _____ May.
d We close every week _____ Wednesday.
e He was born _____ 1998.
f Can you arrange for me to see him _____ July 21st?

Grammar reference

Verb + infinitive with and without *to*

Verb + object + infinitive without *to*

Let and *make* are followed by an object + infinitive without *to*:

Let me know about the meeting.
It **makes you think.**

Verb + object + infinitive with *to*

Allow, get, persuade, want, would like are followed by an object + infinitive with *to*:

He **allowed me to come.**
They **got me to sign** immediately.
She **persuaded me to come.**

Verb + infinitive with *to*

Need, want, would like, would love, regret are followed by an infinitive with *to*:

We **need to buy** some new equipment.
I **want to see** you as soon as possible.
I **would like to know** more about it.

Choose the correct alternative in these sentences.

a Let me (to know / know) when they arrive.
b Do you need (to order / order) them now?
c He'd like (to learn / learn) Spanish.
d He makes us (to work / work) hard.
e I would like them (to do / do) it if they can.
f He persuaded me (to ask / ask) for less.

Irregular verbs

be	was, were	been
become	became	become
begin	began	begun
bet	bet	bet
break	broke	broken
bring	brought	brought
buy	bought	bought
choose	chose	chosen
come	came	come
cost	cost	cost
cut	cut	cut
do	did	done
drink	drank	drunk
drive	drove	driven
eat	ate	eaten
fall	fell	fallen
feel	felt	felt
find	found	found
fly	flew	flown
forget	forgot	forgotten
get	got	got
give	gave	given
go	went	gone
have	had	had
hear	heard	heard
keep	kept	kept
know	knew	known
lead	led	led
learn	learnt / learned	learnt / learned
leave	left	left
lend	lent	lent
let	let	let
lose	lost	lost
make	made	made
mean	meant	meant
meet	met	met
pay	paid	paid
put	put	put
read	read	read
ring	rang	rung
run	ran	run
say	said	said
see	saw	seen
sell	sold	sold
send	sent	sent
show	showed	shown
shut	shut	shut
sing	sang	sung
sit	sat	sat
speak	spoke	spoken
spell	spelt / spelled	spelt / spelled
spend	spent	spent
split	split	split
stand	stood	stood
steal	stole	stolen
swim	swam	swum
take	took	taken
teach	taught	taught
tell	told	told
think	thought	thought
understand	understood	understood
wear	wore	worn
win	won	won
write	wrote	written

accommodation /əkɒmə'deɪʃn/ a place to live, work, or stay, e.g. a hotel

an account /ə'kaʊnt/ a financial arrangement with a bank or company

accounting /ə'kaʊntɪŋ/ keeping and checking accounts

an acknowledgement /ək'nɒlɪdʒmənt/ a letter or telephone call to say that something has been received

an adjustment /ə'dʒʌstmənt/ a change (in figures) to make something correct

administration /ədmɪnɪ'streɪʃn/ the routine organization of a business

to advertise /'ædvətaɪz/ to publicize, give information to the public

an advertisement /əd'vɜːtɪsmənt/ publicity in newspaper, TV, etc. offering (or asking for) a product or service; sometimes abbreviated to *advert* or *ad*

to afford /ə'fɔːd/ to have enough money to pay for something

an agent /'eɪdʒənt/ someone who finds customers for another person, often in a different country

an agreement /ə'griːmənt/ a promise or contract between people or organizations

an answerphone /'ɑːnsəfəʊn/ a telephone, or machine attached to one, that can answer calls automatically and record messages left by the caller

to apologize /ə'pɒlədʒaɪz/ to say you are sorry

applicable /'æplɪkəbl/ relevant

an application /æplɪ'keɪʃn/ a formal request for something, e.g. a job, a bank account

to apply for /ə'plaɪ/ to ask for something, e.g. a job, a place on a course

an appointment /ə'pɔɪntmənt/ a meeting that has been arranged for a particular date and time

approval /ə'pruːvl/ acceptance of something

to approve /ə'pruːv/ to say that something is acceptable

to arrange /ə'reɪndʒ/ to organize

an arrangement /ə'reɪndʒmənt/ a plan, or preparations for a future event

the asking price /'ɑːskɪŋ praɪs/ the price at which something is offered for sale; the seller may be willing to accept less

available /ə'veɪləbl/ not busy, free to talk (of people); ready for immediate sale (of products)

a bank /bæŋk/ institution which holds money on behalf of its customers

to bank /bæŋk/ to deposit money in a bank account

a bargain /'bɑːgɪn/ something that is sold below the asking price

to bargain /'bɑːgɪn/ to ask the seller to lower the price

to bear (the) cost /beə ðə kɒst/ to be responsible for payment

a benchmark /'bentʃmɑːk/ a reference point, or standard, for measuring the quality of other items

a bill /bɪl/ a written list of money owed for goods or services; see **invoice**

a boardroom /'bɔːdruːm/ a room where directors of a company have meetings

capital /'kæpɪtl/ money used to start a business or which belongs to a business

to charge /tʃɑːdʒ/ to ask for payment for goods or a service

to chase (up) payment /tʃeɪs 'peɪmənt/ to ask the person or company which owes money to pay

a cheque /tʃek/ a special printed form for transferring money from one bank account to another, which is signed by the account holder

to clear /klɪə/ to pay (a bill, a debt)

a client /'klaɪənt/ someone who buys a service; see **customer**

a colleague /'kɒliːg/ someone who works with you in the same organization

commerce /'kɒmɜːs/ buying and selling goods and services, and all the activities related to this; see **trade**

a commissioner /kə'mɪʃənə/ an official in a commission (government department)

communication /kəmjuːnɪ'keɪʃn/ exchange of information between people

communications /kəmjuːnɪ'keɪʃnz/ systems which allow transport of goods and people

a company /'kʌmpəni/ an organization that makes, buys, or sells goods, or offers a service for profit

to compensate /'kɒmpənseɪt/ to pay money (or goods) to someone whose property has been damaged or lost

a competitor /kəm'petɪtə/ a person (or company) that works in the same market

to complain /kəm'pleɪn/ to say you are unhappy about goods or a service

a complaint /kəm'pleɪnt/ a statement from someone who is complaining

conditions /kən'dɪʃənz/ terms in a contract or agreement

a conference /'kɒnfərəns/ a meeting or series of meetings, for a group of people with a common interest, e.g. a sales conference in a company

to confirm /kən'fɜːm/ to say that something is correct

a consignee /kɒnsaɪ'niː/ a customer, person receiving goods

a consignment /kən'saɪnmənt/ a quantity of goods sent to a customer or agent

consignment note /kən'saɪnmənt ˌnəʊt/ a document sent with goods with details about the goods and sender / consignor, and signed by the consignee on arrival

a consignor /kən'saɪnə/ a person sending goods to a customer

a container /kən'teɪnə/ a box or bottle, etc. in which goods are transported and sold

convenient /kən'viːnjənt/ suitable, e.g. a *convenient* time for a meeting

correspondence /kɒrɪs'pɒndəns/ communication in writing (letters, faxes, etc.)

the cost /kɒst/ the amount of money you pay for something

to cost /kɒst/ to be the price of a product or service

costing /'kɒstɪŋ/ a breakdown of what something will cost

cost price /'kɒst ˌpraɪs/ the price you pay when you buy goods to resell at a higher price

a courier /'kʊrɪə/ a person or company that delivers goods quickly

current /'kʌrənt/ happening now, e.g. a current price list has today's prices

a CV (curriculum vitae) /siː viː/ a document which summarizes a person's education, qualifications, and work experience

credit /'kredɪt/ an arrangement where goods or services can be paid for later

a customer /'kʌstəmə/ a person or organization that buys goods or services

customer base /'kʌstəmə ˌbeɪs/ regular customers

customs /'kʌstəmz/ (7A) habits, or behaviour which is usual in certain cultures; (9A) the place where goods are examined before export or import

Glossary

a **deadline** /'dedlaɪn/ the time and date when something must be completed

to **deal with** /'di:l ˌwɪð/ to give your attention to something or someone, often to solve a problem; to do business with; to discuss

a **debt** /det/ money that is owed

to **deduct** /dɪ'dʌkt/ to take away an amount of money from a bigger amount

to **deliver** /dɪ'lɪvə/ to take goods, etc. to where they are wanted

a **demand** /dɪ'mɑ:nd/ a strong request e.g. for payment; a product or service which is wanted by the public is *in demand*

a **deposit** /dɪ'pɒsɪt/ payment of part of a larger sum of money

a **depot** /'depəʊ/ a place where goods are stored while being transferred from one place to another

a **design** /dɪ'zaɪn/ how something looks or works; a drawing that shows this; a new design can be a product that is given new characteristics

a **destination** /destɪ'neɪʃn/ the place where people or goods go; the end of a journey

a **discount** /'dɪskaʊnt/ a reduction in price

to **dispatch** /dɪs'pætʃ/ to send goods, letters, etc. (also: *despatch*)

to **disregard** /dɪsrəgɑ:d/ not to take into consideration; ignore

a **display** /dɪs'pleɪ/ an arrangement of goods for sale in a place where people can see them

a **distributor** /dɪs'trɪbjʊtə/ a person or organization that supplies goods to shops from the producer or manufacturer

a **document** /'dɒkjʊmənt/ a written or printed paper that records an agreement or event, or gives proof of identification or ownership

documentary credit /dɒkjʊˌmentrɪ 'kredɪt/ a letter of credit to which an exporter attaches other documents (e.g. a Bill of Lading, an insurance certificate) to obtain payment from a bank

a **draft** /drɑ:ft/ an early version of a letter / document; a bank draft

to **earn** /ɜ:n/ to make money by working or from investments

efficient /ɪ'fɪʃənt/ when a system, machine, or person produces good results quickly

to **employ** /ɪm'plɔɪ/ to give work to someone: an employer gives work to an employee

to **enclose** /ɪn'kləʊz/ to include something in an envelope with a letter

engaged /ɪn'geɪdʒd/ busy (on the phone)

an **enquiry** /ɪn'kwaɪrɪ/ a question you ask to get information (also: *inquiry*)

equipment /ɪ'kwɪpmənt/ the things used for a particular job or hobby

to **estimate** /'estɪmeɪt/ to give an approximate cost or value of something

EU /i: ju:/ the European Union

to **exchange** /ɪks'tʃeɪndʒ/ to give or receive goods or money, etc. for something of equal value

expense /ɪk'spens/ money spent by someone while doing a job

an **expiry date** /ɪk'spaɪrɪ ˌdeɪt/ the date after which something is no longer valid

an **export agency** /'ekspɔ:t ˌeɪdʒənsɪ/ a business that promotes the export of goods or services

to **export** /ɪk'spɔ:t/ to send goods or services into another country

an **exporter** /ɪk'spɔ:tə/ the person or organization that exports goods

an **extension number** /ɪk'stenʃn ˌnʌmbə/ a telephone number inside a company to which you can be connected from a switchboard

facilities /fə'sɪlətɪz/ equipment, rooms, services e.g. *conference facilities* might include a flip-chart and an overhead projector

faulty goods /fɔ:ltɪ 'gʊdz/ goods that are damaged or imperfect

a **fax** /fæks/ a copy of a document sent or received electronically through telephone lines

a **fee** /fi:/ money paid for a professional service

a **file** /faɪl/ a collection of information or documents kept in a particular place; containers for keeping documents

to **fill in** /ˌfɪl 'ɪn/ to complete something, often a pre-printed form

financial /faɪ'nænʃl/ to do with money

a **flight** /flaɪt/ a journey on a plane

a **flow chart** /'fləʊ ˌtʃɑ:t/ a diagram, which is often used in business, to show the stages of a process and how long they take

a **font** /fɒnt/ a typeface

a **fortune** /'fɔ:tʃu:n/ a lot of money

a **forwarding company** /'fɔ:wədɪŋ ˌkʌmpənɪ/ a company that organizes the transportation of goods

franchising /'fræntʃaɪzɪŋ/ an agreement where a franchisee buys the right to use a franchisor's trade name

free /fri:/ something which you don't need to pay for; someone who is not busy at the moment

free of charge /fri: əv tʃɑ:dʒ/ for no payment

freight /freɪt/ the transportation of goods from one place to another by sea or air; goods transported in this way

full-time /fʊl taɪm/ for all the normal working hours in a week

a **function** /'fʌŋkʃn/ an event

a **garment** /'gɑ:mənt/ an item of clothing, usually when talking about the manufacture or sale of clothes

to **get through** /ˌget 'θru:/ to make contact with someone on the telephone

a **gift** /gɪft/ a present

to **give away** /ˌgɪv ə'weɪ/ to give free without charging

to **go ahead with** /ˌgəʊ ə'hed wɪð/ to continue with something

to **go in with** /ˌgəʊ 'ɪn wɪð/ to do something with other people

goods /gʊdz/ manufactured products for sale

gross /grəʊs/ total cost / price / weight etc. before discount

guarantee /gærən'ti:/ to promise (vb); a written promise (n)

handcrafted /'hænd ˌkrɑ:ftɪd/ made by hand

to **handle** /'hændl/ to deal with

handling /'hændlɪŋ/ moving, packing, storing goods

to **hold** /həʊld/ to wait (on the phone)

to **import** /ɪm'pɔ:t/ to bring goods or services into a country

an **importer** /ɪm'pɔ:tə/ the person or organization that imports things

in charge of /ɪn 'tʃɑ:dʒ əv/ responsible for

income /'ɪnkʌm/ money received

incoterms /ˈɪnkəʊtɜːmz/ words used to describe transport and insurance costs (issued by the International Chamber of Commerce), used in international trade contracts; the incoterms used in this book are listed here

Air Waybill (AWB) /eəˈweɪ bɪl / a document that accompanies goods when they are transported by air

Bill of Lading /bɪl əv ˈleɪdɪŋ/ a document that gives details of goods that are being transported

CIF /siː aɪ ef/ an export price which includes cost, insurance, and freight

ex-works /eks wɜːks/ delivery takes place at the seller's factory; the buyer pays for transit costs and takes the risk

FOB /ef eʊ biː/ free on board, an export price that does not include the cost of shipping

SAD /es eɪ diː/ Single Administrative Document: the customs document used in Europe

industry /ˈɪndʌstrɪ/ the production of goods or services to sell

an **in-service course** /ˈɪnsɜːvɪs ˌkɔːs/ a training course in specific skills for people who already work for a company

insurance /ɪnˈʃʊərəns/ a system of guarding against loss, damage, or injury to property and people by paying money to a company that agrees to pay for repairs or replace property that is damaged or stolen

to **invest** /ɪnˈvest/ to put money into a business with the hope of making a profit

an **investment** /ɪnˈvestmənt/ the money put into a business

an **invoice** /ˈɪnvɔɪs/ a list of goods or services sold and of how much must be paid for them; see **bill**

to **invoice** /ˈɪnvɔɪs/ to send or prepare an invoice

IT /aɪ tiː/ information technology, e.g. the IT department of a company

an **irrevocable letter of credit** /ˈɪrevəkəbl ˌletə(r) əv ˈkredɪt/ a letter of credit which can only be cancelled with the agreement of the payee

an **item** /ˈaɪtəm/ a thing, e.g. items in a list

to **itemize** /ˈaɪtəmaɪz/ to separate or specify every item on a bill or list

a **label** /ˈleɪbl/ the name of the producer of

particular products; a piece of paper, etc. that is attached to a product and gives information about it

layout /ˈleɪaʊt/ the position and design of words and pictures in e.g. a letter or newspaper

a **leaflet** /ˈliːflət/ a piece of printed paper that provides information or advertises something

legal /ˈliːgl/ allowed by the law

a **letter of credit** /ˈletə(r) əv ˈkredɪt/ a letter that is sent from one bank to another so that a customer can get money

letterhead /ˈletəhed/ the part of a letter with the printed name, address, and logo of an organization or company

liable for /ˈlaɪəbl/ responsible for paying a debt or making good damage or loss

literature /ˈlɪtrətʃə/ printed information about a product or service, e.g. brochures, leaflets, and catalogues

a **loan** /ləʊn/ money lent on condition that it will be paid back at a later date, usually with interest

a **logo** /ˈləʊgəʊ/ a symbol or design used on products, buildings, stationery, etc. to advertise a company

a **loss** /lɒs/ money lost in business; when a company gets back less than it invests, it *makes a loss*

Ltd (Limited) /ˈlɪmɪtɪd/ private limited company (in the UK); a company which is owned by its members, and which cannot offer its shares for sale

mail order /ˌmeɪl ˈɔːdə/ buying and selling by post

to **manage** /ˈmænɪdʒ/ to be in charge or in control of something

a **manager** /ˈmænɪdʒə/ a person involved in managing something

manufacturing industries /mænjʊˈfæktʃərɪŋ ˌɪndʌstrɪz/ factories producing large quantities of goods with machinery

marketing /ˈmɑːkɪtɪŋ/ the activity of identifying potential buyers for a product and stimulating a demand

market research /ˌmɑːkɪt riːˈsɜːtʃ/ studying a market to discover facts about it

a **meeting** /ˈmiːtɪŋ/ an organized occasion when people get together to discuss / decide something

a **mission statement** /ˈmɪʃn ˌsteɪtmənt/ a statement of the objectives and policy of an organization

a **module** /ˈmɒdjʊl/ part of a course

a **motif** /məʊˈtiːf/ a design

notification /nəʊtɪfɪˈkeɪʃn/ the process of informing somebody about something (formal)

to **notify** /ˈnəʊtɪfaɪ/ to inform somebody about something (formal)

on behalf of /ɒn bɪˈhɑːf əv/ for somebody / an organization

an **operator** /ˈɒpəreɪtə/ someone who works at a telephone switchboard, or controls a machine

an **option** /ˈɒpʃn/ the right to sell or buy something at an agreed amount

an **order** /ˈɔːdə/ a request for goods to be supplied or made; the goods supplied

to **order** /ˈɔːdə/ to ask for something to be supplied or made

an **outcome** /ˈaʊtkʌm/ a result

an **outlet** /ˈaʊtlet/ a place where goods are sold to the public, e.g. a shop

outstanding /aʊtˈstændɪŋ/ unpaid

overdue /əʊvədjuː/ late

overleaf /əʊvəˈliːf/ on the other side of a piece of paper

overtime /ˈəʊvətaɪm/ work that is extra to the usual working time

to **owe** /əʊ/ to be in debt to

an **owner** /ˈəʊnə/ the person to whom something belongs

a **PA** /piː eɪ/ a personal assistant to a manager

a **pack** /pæk/ things that are sold or given together, e.g. an *information pack*

to **pack** /pæk/ to put in containers to sell or transport

a **package** /ˈpækɪdʒ/ a number of things packed together

packaging /ˈpækɪdʒɪŋ/ materials that protect products during transportation

a **partner** /ˈpɑːtnə/ one of two or more people who own or run a business together

a **partnership** /ˈpɑːtnəʃɪp/ an association of two or more people who own or run a

Glossary

business together

part-time /ˈpɑːtˌtaɪm/ working for only part of the full working week

a **pattern** /ˈpætn/ a design

payable /ˈpeɪəbl/ that should be paid

a **payee** /peɪˈiː/ the person who receives a payment, e.g. a cheque or letter of credit

a **payment** /ˈpeɪmənt/ an amount of money to be paid

percentage /pəˈsentɪdʒ/ part of a hundred; 100% is the total amount

performance /pəˈfɔːməns/ the way something is done

perishables /ˈperɪʃəblz/ goods, like food, that go bad (perish) quickly

a **personal organizer** /ˌpɜːsənl ˈɔːgənaɪzə/ a kind of diary which you can add pages to or remove pages from

a **plan** /plæn/ a detailed drawing of a building; an arrangement

PLC /piː el siː/ public limited company (in the UK); a company which can sell its shares to the public

policy /ˈpɒləsɪ/ a plan of action; a description of a company's position on an important issue

a **postal order** /ˈpəʊstl ˌɔːdə/ a piece of paper bought from a post office which represents the amount of money paid for it and which can be exchanged for cash by the person who receives it and is named on it

prepaid /ˌpriːˈpeɪd/ paid in advance

a **presentation** /ˌpreznˈteɪʃn/ an occasion when someone talks about or presents something at a meeting

a **price** /praɪs/ the amount of money that something costs

a **product** /ˈprɒdʌkt/ something that is made to sell

production /prəˈdʌkʃn/ the activity of producing; a theatrical show

a **profit** /ˈprɒfɪt/ the money made by / from a business

profitable /ˈprɒfɪtəbl/ making money by selling goods or services

a **proforma invoice** /prəʊˌfɔːmə ˈɪnvɔɪs/ an invoice that is sent before the goods are supplied

to **promote** /prəˈməʊt/ to advertise; to give someone a more important job in a company

a **proof** /pruːf/ a copy of something printed to show what it will finally look like

property /ˈprɒpətɪ/ things people own; land and buildings

a **proposal** /prəˈpəʊzl/ a suggested idea or plan for people to consider

publicity /pʌbˈlɪsətɪ/ attracting people's attention by giving information about something, often with the intention of selling it

public relations /ˌpʌblɪk rɪˈleɪʃnz/ the job of giving information about a company to help maintain or improve its public image

publishing /ˈpʌblɪʃɪŋ/ preparing and printing books / newspapers / etc.

to **purchase** /ˈpɜːtʃɪs/ to buy something (formal)

to **put through** /ˌpʊt ˈθruː/ to connect two people on the telephone

quality /ˈkwɒlətɪ/ how good something is; the condition of something

a **quantity** /ˈkwɒntətɪ/ an amount

quarter /ˈkwɔːtə/ three months of a year; 25% of something

a **questionnaire** /ˌkwestʃəˈneə/ a list of questions for people to answer, e.g. when doing market research

a **quotation** /kwəʊˈteɪʃn/ the price given for some work or a service before it is done

to **raise cash** /ˌreɪz ˈkæʃ/ to obtain money

a **range** /reɪndʒ/ a group or collection of similar products

a **receipt** /rɪˈsiːt/ a document that shows that goods have been paid for; *on receipt*: when you receive

a **recipient** /rɪˈsɪpɪənt/ someone who receives something

redundant /rɪˈdʌndənt/ no longer needed; a person who *is made redundant* loses his / her job

a **reference** /ˈrefərəns/ a letter from a previous employer about the quality of your work and personality

a **refund** /ˈriːfʌnd/ money given back

to **regret** /rɪˈgret/ to be sorry

to **reject** /rɪˈdʒekt/ to say no to something

a **repayment** /rɪˈpeɪmənt/ money given back, e.g. because goods are faulty

a **replacement** /rɪˈpleɪsmənt/ a substitute for something that is damaged or wrong

in **reply** /ˌɪn rɪˈplaɪ/ in answer

to **request** /rɪˈkwest/ to ask for

to **require** /rɪˈkwaɪə/ to need; to ask for

a **requirement** /rɪˈkwaɪəmənt/ something that is needed or asked for

a **reservation** /ˌrezəˈveɪʃn/ a booking

to **retail** /ˈriːteɪl/ to sell to the general public

a **retail chain** /ˈriːteɪl ˌtʃeɪn/ a chain of shops owned by the same company

a **retailer** /ˈriːteɪlə/ a person or company that sells directly to the public

a **risk** /rɪsk/ you *take a risk* when you do something that may not be successful

a **rubber band** /ˌrʌbə ˈbænd/ a thin circle of elastic rubber used to hold things together

to **run** /rʌn/ to *run* a company or office means to manage it

a **safe** /seɪf/ a strong box with a key for keeping money, etc. secure

a **salary** /ˈsælərɪ/ regular payment for work done for a company

a **sales department** /ˈseɪlz dɪˌpɑːtmənt/ the part of a company responsible for selling goods or services

a **sample** /ˈsɑːmpl/ an example of a product

to **schedule** /ˈʃedjuːl/ to programme; *to reschedule* is to change the time of an arrangement

a **selling point** /ˈselɪŋ ˌpɔɪnt/ a special feature of a product that will make people want to buy it

selling price /ˈselɪŋ ˌpraɪs/ the cost of goods to the general public

a **service** /ˈsɜːvɪs/ the work or job that a non-manufacturing company does; an organization that helps with something useful, e.g. the health service

a **share** /ʃeə/ a part; a company's capital can be divided into shares, and the people who have the shares are shareholders in the company and can vote on important decisions

to **share** /ʃeə/ to divide something between a number of people

a **shelf** /ʃelf/ plural: *shelves*; a surface where things are kept, e.g. a book shelf

to **ship** /ʃɪp/ to send products by sea or air

a **shipment** /ˈʃɪpmənt/ a quantity of goods being shipped

a **shipping company** /ˈʃɪpɪŋ ˌkʌmpənɪ/ an organization that arranges for goods to be sent to another country by sea, air, rail, or road

shipping documents /ˈʃɪpɪŋ ˌdɒkjʊmənts/ the documents sent by an exporter to a bank or agent in the importer's country, e.g. a bill of lading, an insurance certificate, a certificate of origin, an export licence

to **shortlist** /ˈʃɔːtlɪst/ to select a small number of people from a large number of people who have applied for a job

a **signature** /ˈsɪɡnɪtʃə/ a handwritten name on a letter or document

a **slogan** /ˈsləʊɡən/ a memorable expression associated with a company or one of its products

a **sole trader** /ˌsəʊl ˈtreɪdə/ a person who owns and runs a business by him / herself

a **solicitor** /səˈlɪsɪtə/ a lawyer (in the UK; *attorney* in the USA)

speedy /ˈspiːdi/ fast

to **spend** /spend/ to pay money for something you want

staff /stɑːf/ the people who work for a company

a **stage** /steɪdʒ/ a part of an activity, e.g. a phone conversation

a **stand** /stænd/ a stall or shop at a trade fair

to **stand out** /ˌstænd ˈaʊt/ to be noticeable

to **state** /steɪt/ to say (formal)

a **statement** /ˈsteɪtmənt/ a list of amounts paid and owed, that a seller sends a buyer, usually every month

stationery /ˈsteɪʃənri/ writing materials, e.g. paper, envelopes, pens

statistics /stəˈtɪstɪks/ information presented in a numerical form

in **stock** /ˌɪn ˈstɒk/ available for sale

a **storeroom** /ˈstɔːˌruːm/ a place where goods are kept

to **submit** /səbˈmɪt/ to give something to someone for consideration or for action

a **supplier** /səˈplaɪə/ the person or company that gives goods or services to a shop or another company

to **supply** /səˈplaɪ/ to give goods *(supplies)* to a customer

support /səˈpɔːt/ help, assistance

a **switchboard** /ˈswɪtʃbɔːd/ equipment used for receiving and transferring telephone calls in a company

time out /ˈtaɪm ˌaʊt/ a break from a job or activity

a **tip** /tɪp/ a suggestion

tourism /ˈtʊərɪzm/ the industry that provides accommodation, transport, etc. for people who travel for pleasure

a **track record** /ˌtræk ˈrekɔːd/ the success, or lack of it, of a business or person in business over a period of time

trade /treɪd/ buying and selling

a **trade fair** /ˈtreɪd ˌfeə/ an exhibition where manufacturers and sellers display their goods to potential customers

training /ˈtreɪnɪŋ/ teaching people how to do a particular job

transport /ˈtrɑːnspɔːt/ movement of people or goods from one place to another by car / train / etc.

a **trip** /trɪp/ a short journey you make to another place and back again, often for business

unbeatable /ʌnˈbiːtəbl/ when no one can do better, e.g. *an unbeatable offer*

unconditional /ˌʌnkənˈdɪʃənl/ absolute

to **undertake** /ˌʌndəˈteɪk/ to agree to do something

unsaleable /ʌnˈseɪləbl/ goods which are *unsaleable* cannot be sold, usually because they are of poor quality or damaged

up-to-date /ˌʌptəˈdeɪt/ modern, following the most recent ideas

valid /ˈvælɪd/ legally acceptable

of **value** /ˈvæljuː/ worth a lot

VAT /viː eɪ tiː/ Value Added Tax (in the UK); tax on goods which are sold

a **voucher** /ˈvaʊtʃə/ a piece of paper that can be exchanged for goods or services for the amount shown

a **warehouse** /ˈweəhaʊs/ a large building where goods are stored

wholesaler /ˈhəʊlseɪlə/ a person or company that buys in large quantities from the manufacturer and sells to the retailer

will /wɪl/ a legal document that states what must happen to someone's money and property after his / her death

wrapping /ˈræpɪŋ/ the material used for covering or packing goods

Oxford University Press,
Great Clarendon Street, Oxford OX2 6DP

Oxford   New York
Auckland Bangkok Buenos Aires
Cape Town Chennai Dar es Salaam
Delhi Hong Kong Istanbul Karachi
Kolkata Kuala Lumpur Madrid
Melbourne Mexico City Mumbai
Nairobi São Paulo Shanghai Taipei
Tokyo Toronto

OXFORD and OXFORD ENGLISH
are trade marks of Oxford University Press

ISBN 0 19 457230 7

© Oxford University Press 1999
Eighth impression 2003

No unauthorized photocopying

Typeset by Oxford University Press
Printed in China

Acknowledgements
The authors and publisher are grateful to those who have given permission to reproduce the following extracts and adaptations of copyright material:

p 14 Extracts from London Facts and Figures (1995 edition). HMSO Copyright Unit. Crown copyright is reproduced with the permission of the Controller of Her Majesty's Stationery Office.

p 15 1991 Census, Small Area Statistics Table 2: Age Groups in Highbury Vale. OPCS Crown Copyright. Crown copyright is reproduced with the permission of the Controller of Her Majesty's Stationery Office.

p 27 Philosophy Football, PO Box 10684, London N15 6XA. (NB Prices not actual.)

pp 34, 38, 40 Tees Total for use of adapted letter, order form, and special offer information.

p 35 Jarvis Hotels for use of extracts from 'Summit Conferences': Jarvis International Gatwick Brochure (newest edition 1998). (NB Prices not actual.)

p 36 Just For You for use of adapted promotional material.

p 46 Extracts from article by Peter Cochrane, with his permission. Full version of article first appeared in WIRED UK, June 1995.

p 64 Extracts from *Running a Home Based Business* by Diane M. Baker published by Kogan Page. Reproduced by permission of Kogan Page Limited/Earthscan Publications Limited.

p 81 Yogen Früz Canada Inc. for use of Bresler's Ice Cream & Yogurt Shops Franchise Information taken from the Internet.

The publisher would like to thank the following for permission to reproduce photographs:

Ace Photo Agency p 78 (R Altman).

Britstock p 57.

Ikea Ltd p 21.

The Image Bank p 14 (Oxford Street/D&G Bowater), 60 (Man on phone/S Niedorf).

The NEC Group, Birmingham p 26.

Network Photographers p 83.

Past Times p 21 (umbrella stand).

Pictor p 48.

Sony p 20.

Telegraph Colour Library p 14 (web press/L Lefkowitz), 24 (man on phone), 56 (Lorries/D Noton).

Tony Stone Images p 14 (Waterloo/C Kapolka), 24 (Secretary/J Riley), 37 (S Peters), 56 (freight train/ K Blaxland), (Air Cargo), (ship).

World Pictures p 44.

We would also like to thank Eastnor Pottery for permission to photograph products.

Cover photograph by:
Telegraph Colour Library/B Cannizaro; (woman using mobile)

Illustrations by:
Harry Venning pp 9, 12, 13, 14, 22, 25, 41, 43, 45, 51, 54, 55, 59, 61, 62.

Ned Jolliffe pp 29, 84.

Technical Graphics Dept, OUP pp 6, 7.

Location and studio photography by:
Trevor Clifford pp 6, 7, 8, 12, 13, 17, 18, 19, 20, 23, 24, 27, 33, 36, 37, 38, 42, 50, 51, 60, 62, 66, 67, 69, 70, 72, 73, 75, 79, 80, 82.

Mark Mason pp 31, 76.

The authors and publisher would like to thank the teachers and students of the following institutions for their advice and assistance in the preparation of this book:

France: Institut AR CA, Evry; ISEG, Nantes; Lycée Emile Dubois, Paris; Lycée Haute-Follis, Laval; Lycée Jacques Prevert, Longjuneau; Lycée Saint-Exupery, Cretéil

Czech Republic: Eva Vernerova

Hungary: Corvin Mátyás Gimnázium és Müszaki SZKI, Budapest; Közgazdasági Politechnikum, Budapest; Károlyi Mihály Közgazdasági Szakközépiskola, Budapest; Leowey Klara Közgazdasági Szakközépiskola, Budapest; Terézvárosi Kereskedelmi Szakközépiskola, Szondi

Italy: Instituto Professionale per il Commercio e il Turismo, Dalmine; ITC dell'Acqua, Legnano; ITC Duca degli Abruzzi Rieti; ITC Arduino, Turin; IPC Strampelli, Rieti; ITC Piaggia, Viareggio

Poland: Zespó Szkó Handlowych, Bydgoszcz; Zespó Szkó Ekonomiczno-Administracyjnych, Bydgoszcz; Zespól Szkól Elektrycznych, Bialystok; Zespó Szkó Energetycznych, Gdaæsk; Zespó Szkól Zawodowych nr 1, E k

Spain: Academia BAI, Madrid; IES Tartanga, Vizcaya; IFP Conselleria, Valencia; Instituto Leonardo da Vinci, Madrid

Turkey: Nilufer Anadolu Ticaret Meslek Lisesi Ihsaniye, Bursa